Childbirth Coaching Guide

S0-AVR-203

Your Role as Her Birth Coach

Real labor is your cue to take charge; be confident, calm and make sure everything she needs gets handled. Be her capable protector who is going to help her get through this. Remain positive for her no matter how you feel.

- **Get ready early:** Once labor starts, check your lists and make sure everything is packed and ready to go.

- **Make the calls & check her in:** Call the doctor, handle the paperwork and any hassles at the hospital.

- **Manage communications:** With the nursing and medical staff, ask questions and get answers.

- **Present your birth plan:** To the labor nurse on each shift and remind them of its core elements.

- **Support her:** The nurse will come and go and shifts will change; you are the main member of her support team.

- **Manage friends/relatives:** You may need to politely ask visitors to wait outside. The nurse will help.

- **Be flexible:** Deal constructively with new events and changes in course.

- **Handle any tough decisions:** Keep her informed but she may not be lucid when in labor.

- **Listen to her:** If she is shy about making requests, ask her what she wants – regularly.

- **Encourage/reassure her:** Build her confidence, tell her she is doing great, how proud you are of her, you love her.

- **Indulge her:** In any way possible. Pursue her every request regardless of whether you think it is necessary.

- **Take her best shots:** It is the pain and frustration talking. You are helping her blow off steam (and pain).

- **Watch her face:** When you present her your baby to hold for the first time.

Is It Time To Go?

Her contractions are 40-60 seconds long and 5 minutes apart for an hour	She or you are concerned	Water has broken OR Bleeding OR Pain between contractions
Call her physician, report her status and follow instructions	Err on the side of caution and call early, but try to avoid going early to the hospital because being sent home is very frustrating	Call her physician immediately

Be Her Advocate

Only you will know what she really wants, and you need to express her needs to the staff. Intervene and, if necessary, be assertive, such as asking that the anesthesiologist or doctor be paged. Do not lose control and become obnoxious; this will scare her and you will become the problem. Keep her informed and let her wishes guide your actions.

She Needs You

Your presence alone is a major comfort to her as she experiences the surreal, often excruciating experience of birth for the first time. She needs your familiar voice and touch and knowing you care for her more than anyone else.

This is not medical advice; always follow your doctor's instructions

© Dads Adventure 2013

Making A Birth Plan

Birth Plan Summary (Remember To Be Flexible)

Pain Control _____

_____

_____

Labor _____

_____

_____

Monitoring _____

_____

_____

Delivery _____

_____

_____

Dad _____

_____

_____

Post Delivery _____

_____

_____

Breastfeeding _____

_____

_____

Caesarean Birth Basics

About one-third ($^1/_3$) of births in the U.S. involve surgery. Most hospitals allow dads in the operating room for a routine caesarean, and you can still participate by talking to your mate, who may remain awake during the procedure. Tell her that she and the baby will be fine, that you love her, and what is going on, especially after the baby is born. Keep in mind:

- You may be separated from your mate while she is prepped and she may get scared.
- A drape is hung across her chest so she (and you) will not be able to see the actual surgery.
- After birth, your baby's lungs will be suctioned to remove fluid that would be squeezed out during birth.
- You may be offered the opportunity (or ask) to cut the umbilical cord, even though it was already cut during the caesarean birth.
- In a cesarean, the baby is born in the first 5-10 minutes and another 30-45 minutes is spent repairing mom. With her arms under the surgical drape, she cannot hold her baby.
- Hold your baby close to her face so she can look him in the eyes, touch him and say hello. Then you hold him skin-to-skin, look him in the eyes and welcome him.
- If he is taken to be checked and cleaned, go with the baby (or carry him), and keep mom informed. If taken to another room, tell her you are going with him and will be back.

Her hospital stay will be longer, providing you many opportunities to learn how to care for your baby from the nurses as well as great bonding time alone with your new family. Of course, her recovery will require weeks, and you will need to fill the gap.

If Problems Develop

If things aren't going as planned the doctor might suggest an intervention, ranging from the use of forceps to a caesarean birth. If it's an emergency, there will probably be no time for consideration, but if it's not, you can ask questions such as:
- ❑ What are the benefits?
- ❑ What are the risks?
- ❑ What are the alternatives?
- ❑ Does your intuition say 'go for it'?
- ❑ Does it need to be done Now, or can it wait?

If a problem develops:
- ❑ Trust your doctors; they are highly trained and in emergency situations, time is of the essence.
- ❑ Stay calm, ask questions of medical staff, and let them do their jobs.
- ❑ Keep mom informed and reassured.

While your own feelings can be overwhelming, your response to the needs of your family at this critical time will be crucial. Hang in there. This is when a new baby really needs his father.

> While they were stitching my wife up, I went to the changing table with the nurse and my baby. I was the first voice that she really heard, and when I opened up, she zoned right in on me. That was probably the most heart melting moment I've ever had."
> — Veteran Dad

This is not medical advice; always follow your doctor's instructions

© Dads Adventure 2013

Coaching Her Through Labor

When Labor Starts

- False labor is frustrating, but will pass.
- Labor is real when her contractions steadily intensify and do not go away if she gets up and changes position.
- She may also develop low back pain; once the real thing kicks in there is no mistaking what it is.

What Is Happening

- Her cervix is gradually effacing (thinning out) and dilating (opening up) to "unplug" her uterus, enabling the baby to pass into the birth canal.
- Her water may break and she may pass the mucus plug.

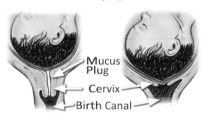

Mucus Plug
Cervix
Birth Canal

Early Labor

Labor averages 15 hours for first time moms, with about half that time spent at home, which is more comfortable than a hospital room.

- Encourage her to relax, sleep, talk, walk, take a bath (get a quick shower yourself), watch a movie, or snuggle (these last hours together before you become parents can be very special).
- Try to get her mind off her labor and save her energy for later as it gets more intense.
- Encourage her to eat, drink fluids and go to the bathroom.

Drive Her Carefully

Check your list and load the car. This is no NASCAR event; drive as smoothly as possible since sudden moves and even small bumps on the road are a shock to a woman in labor. An easy drive also helps mom stay calm and focused.

Log Contractions

Handle early contractions by getting her to ignore them as much as possible (also delay the use of labor techniques until they are necessary). Use this log to track the progress of labor and what helps her get through it. First track contractions until labor is clearly underway, and then periodically to see how she is progressing. Comment about which techniques work and what else is going on. You can also use www.contractionmaster.com or a smartphone app.

Start/Time	Length	Time Apart	Comments/ What's happening?
5:32:26	48 sec		This is starting to happen!
5:39:42	50 sec	7:16 min	Breathing, helped her get through it

Hospital Information

Doctor's Name _____ Phone # _____

Hospital Phone _____ Other _____

When to call/go: _____

_____

This is not medical advice; always follow your doctor's instructions

Help Her Deal With Pain

Pain Medication: Yes, No, Maybe?

Her method for dealing with pain is her call. If she wants an epidural, urge that it be provided as early as possible and don't expect it to eliminate all her pain. Use basic pain control techniques to help her. If she wants to go without pain meds, support her in every way possible. If she has trouble tolerating the pain early in labor, encourage her to consider medication because it may become much worse. If it is late in her labor, remind her how far along she is and encourage her to stick it out. This way she will know she gave it her best shot. Then follow her wishes, and if she requests an epidural, ask that it be administered immediately. Also ask about the point when it would be too late for her to obtain one.

Focus on Her

Count her through contractions; let her know when the monitor indicates they peak. Ask the nurse what to look for so you can alert her if necessary. Not a good time to get fascinated with machines, though. Same with your role as cameraman; take a few pictures but keep the focus on mom.

Engage Her Directly

❑ Get hands-on; hold her gently, caress her head, massage her, get whisper-close to her face.
❑ Talk her through each contraction; pace her breathing, tell her when it peaks, when it is done.
❑ Start breathing with her and if she falters, encourage her to "breathe with me, there you go, stay with it now, hang in there, it's starting to peak, it's on the way down, that's it baby."
❑ You may need to get face-to-face to get her focus back. Calmly but firmly, tell her to "look at me, stay with me, I love you and am going to help you get through this, now breathe with me."
❑ Once a contraction ends, help her relax. Ask her if she wants anything else, and depending on how it is going, suggest a different position, breathing pattern, or whatever you think might work.

Common Labor Terms

Dilation: Width in centimeters of opening in the cervix, with 10 cms (4 inches) required for birth.
Effacement: Flatness of the cervix represented by a percent.
Position: Way the baby is facing.
Presentation: Part of the baby coming first.
Station: How far down the first part of the baby is in the birth canal, on a scale of -5 to +5.
Crowning: When Baby's head begins to appear before birth.
Apgar Score: A nurse evaluates your baby 1 and 5 minutes after birth on five characteristics like breathing and skin color giving each a score between 0 and 2. A total score of 7+ indicates your baby is doing well; less than 7 says some added care is needed.

Intense Coaching Time

If she becomes distraught, desperate, despairing, highly stressed, or experiences a high level of pain, it is time for you to take your coaching to the next level to help her regroup. This will be intense, so get in close, stay with her, and do what ever you can that may work. Never give up on her; If you do, you can no longer help her. Project confidence and firmness in your manner, touch and tone of voice. Remember, she will be feeling birth pain for the first time and may react in unexpected ways.

Silence Can Be Best

She may find an intense, inward focus is her best way to get through strong contractions, and telling her how to breathe may break her concentration. If you sense this is the case, just back off.

Call In Reinforcements

If she gives up, tell her you love her, how tough this must be for her, and "we will get through this!" Ask for help from the nurse, who can encourage her, determine her progress, suggest something, or help coach. Tell mom that "your baby is on the way." Always remember she will get through it.

THINGS TO TRY

Soft Music

Research has indicated that soft music can reduce mom's perception of pain in the first hours of active labor, so set her up to listen with an iPod or CD player.

Massage

Massage will help her relax between contractions as well as speed labor along. Ask her where to rub or ask the nurse for ideas. Keep at it but pace yourself.

Childbirth Class Techniques

Use the techniques you learned in childbirth class and try anything else you (or she) thinks might work:
❑ Set up her room with pictures, scented oil, etc.
❑ Help her establish a focal point.
❑ Take her mind off the labor by reading to her, or engaging her mind in other ways.
❑ Try slow dancing with her arms around your neck.
❑ Ask for an exercise ball.
❑ Let her squeeze your hand during contractions.
❑ Suggest she change her breathing pattern.
❑ Encourage her to grunt like a tennis player.
❑ Suggest she lie in different positions.
❑ When she is pushing, work with the nurse to hold her legs in a position that helps her bear down.

Dealing With Back Labor

The hard back of the baby's head may be pushing on mom's spine. Ideas to reduce her pain:
❑ Try a position that moves the baby's head away from her spine, like mom on her hands and knees.
❑ Changing positions, pelvic rocking or squatting may help rotate the baby and relieve the pain.
❑ Strong massage or pushing to create counter pressure where it hurts. Try tennis balls in a sock.
❑ Hot packs, ice, or a warm bath or shower with the water targeting the pain may help.
❑ Ask the nurse or doctor for ideas.

© Dads Adventure 2013

Crash Course for Dads-To-Be

Prepare for the
Adventure of Your Life
with Real World Advice
from Real Dads

Greg Bishop
Founder of Boot Camp for New Dads
and Dads Adventure

Crash Course for Dads-To-Be

Published by
Dads Adventure
Irvine, CA 92618

Copyright © 2013 Greg Bishop

All rights reserved. No part of this book may be reproduced, stored in a retrieval system, or transmitted by any means, electronic, mechanical, photocopying, recording, or otherwise, without written permission from the publisher.

Cover photo – Glen Miller
Design – Autumn Heep
Illustrations – Leanna Cruz

Library of Congress Control Number: 2013932530
ISBN-13: 978-0-9727829-7-5

Information and advice in this book has been carefully researched and every effort has been made to ensure accuracy. Although health care professionals have reviewed pertinent chapters, this book should never substitute for the advice of your personal physician. Dads Adventure assumes no responsibility for any damages or losses incurred as a result of following the information contained herein.

DadsAdventure.com

Crash Course for Dads-To-Be

Ramping Up To Birth

Settling In With Your Baby

Caring For A New Baby

Caring For New Moms

Transforming Into A Dad

Keeping Him Safe And Healthy

Building A Family

Making It An Adventure

Who We Are

My brothers and I grew up taking care of babies. Along with working on cars and fishing for trout, it was just something one did in a family with 13 children. Changing diapers was like cleaning fish; it just went with the territory. So when I became a father myself I knew what to do with our first child, and after four, my friends were asking me for advice on their babies.

I felt most new fathers would enjoy their babies more if they knew what I did, so in 1990, I organized a workshop for dads-to-be at the local hospital. I asked my friends to join me and bring their babies, and for three hours the babies smiled, slept, cried and did what babies do, and the "Rookie" dads-to-be watched us take care of them without a mom in sight. When several said they had never held a baby before, we handed them ours.

Us "Veterans" talked about our experiences and offered advice, and we all got to know and trust each other. Everything said in the room stayed in the room, so nothing was left off the table. The Rookies went home thinking "I can do this," and they did, and returned several months later as Veterans with their own babies to orient the next group of Rookies.

We call it Boot Camp for New Dads (BCND. org), and it has since expanded to 45 states, the U.S. Army, Navy and Air Force, England and Canada. Characterized as a "nursery in a locker room", more than 300,000 men have joined us, just regular guys from all walks of life. We help and encourage each other; in a sense, we act like my brothers and I did growing up.

What We Offer You

This *Crash Course for Dads-To-Be* provides you with a comprehensive orientation on fatherhood from the real experts – men doing the job as new fathers. We have boiled this information (along with the best and latest research) down into a very concise format you will find easy to use, and backed it up with a website offering in-depth supplementary information.

Calling this book a "crash course" may give one the idea it is intended for men who want to take it easy on their road to fatherhood. The opposite is the case; it is intended for men who understand that opportunities for dads abound and that the bar for new fathers has risen considerably. They know that in the few months before their baby arrives, there is a great deal to learn.

There are a variety of tools like the *Childbirth Coaching Guide* you will find very useful, including simple ways to record your thoughts as you transform into a dad over the next year. Fatherhood is a journey and it is helpful to periodically take note of where you are in relation to where you started. We also make it easy for you to pass on what you learn as a new father to the next guy, to help keep the cycle going, by visiting DadsAdventure.com and leaving a comment or sharing a tip.

Please join us in helping each other do our best as fathers. This is our way of making the world a better place for all our children.

Dadsadventure.com Gives You a Great Start

DadsAdventure.com is the supplementary website to Crash Course for Dads-To-Be and provides what you need to know to thrive as a new father. It presents the perspectives of men who have participated in Boot Camp for New Dads as well as related research and information collected over two decades. It is the web's most comprehensive resource for new fathers.

See How-To-Videos Featuring Experienced Dads

Changing diapers, giving baths, calming a crying baby — nothing quite like having another guy show you how, in terms you understand, to give you the confidence that you can do it too. Before long, you will be showing other guys how it is done.

Find Boot Camp for New Dads Workshops in Your Area

Boot Camp for New Dads is acclaimed by virtually all who participate, and if one is located in your community, you will find it enlightening, unique and very worthwhile. For locations, visit DadsAdventure.com or BCND.org.

Find Out How Men Make Fatherhood an Adventure

The ultimate experience in fatherhood is to make it an adventure, and the earlier you start, the better. You will find examples of dads and their kids who are having the times of their life that will give you ideas for your own adventures.

What We Tell Moms-To-Be

Nobody fathers in a vacuum. Check out what we tell the moms-to-be and new moms about men becoming fathers at NewMomsProject.org.

> " I was pretty scared and the class calmed me, so I just want to pay it forward."
> — New Father

Get Downloadable Content

Dads Adventure magazine is for the dad-to-be, and if you did not get one from your hospital, you can download it from DadsAdventure.com, along with other downloads you will find helpful.

Share What You Have Learned with the next Guy

Your experience will be valuable to those who follow you, and you can contribute your own insights to help out the next guy. When it comes to raising our children, we dads are all in this together.

Join Us

We are dads helping each other do our best for our kids, and it would be great to have you with us. There is no formal membership; just learning from the men on the job as fathers, and helping out the next guy in line.

CHAPTER 1

Ramping Up To Birth

"Once the baby's out, it's your turn to shine."
— Veteran Dad

Cave Dads Set the Standard

The caveman has gotten a bad rap due to cheap shots by GEICO. Since he's not around to defend himself, we need to set the record straight:

He was a great dad; placed the bar high for those of us who follow, and equipped and prepared us to clear it.

In pre-historic times, due to a high death rate, many babies were required for the survival of our species. In comparison to other mammals, human babies require a great deal more care, so it took two heads and four hands (and a village). The bottom line, researchers tell us, is that both cave moms and dads were hands-on with their babies in their comfy cave, co-sleeping way before it was cool.

Cave dad no doubt served as a patient punching bag for his mate's developing hormonal surges; this may be when we learned to keep our feelings to ourselves, a lesson a dad-to-be today innately understands. He was also no doubt in awe of the results of these surges: her immense commitment to their baby's survival.

Another mouth to feed meant he hunted down an extra big Mammoth. And when back, his little Neanderthal flashed her

blazingly bright smile, and for some reason he could not comprehend, this aggressive hunter turned to mush.

Naturally strong and courageous, he found himself extra vigilant when his child arrived. A baby attracted saber-tooth cats, but it was no problem, as his protective instincts were supercharged when those pesky felines were around. They made warm baby blankets.

He wrestled and had fun with his kids, and probably listened to mom telling him not to get them worked up before bed time. He taught his children the ways of prehistoric life out in the world and got them ready for when it was time for them to find their own cave.

He passed on to his sons and all of us dads to follow, something very special — an innate drive to protect and care for our children and family, and the instincts to do it well.

> **"** The day after he was born, they took him in to draw his blood. What they don't tell you is how much blood they have to draw and the way they do it. They prick a little hole in his heel and they squeeze. And squeeze. His foot was getting a little blue and he was starting to get more and more upset and ... he had a single tear come down and I was ready to punch the nurse in the face. And that's when I knew. I was like, 'Oh crap. I'm a dad.' I know she was just doing her job, but oh wow, it just gets to you."
>
> — Veteran Dad

So why did this tough, self-centered, survival of the fittest champ settle down and make huge sacrifices for his family? Brain research has given us some answers — turns out that the cave dad was doing R&D and tuning his (our) biology to support a man's transition into the demanding role of dad.

Paternal care is an evolved* behavior in us men. We get a complex, chemical turbo boost, triggered by hands-on contact with our babies that is genetically programmed to kick start our daddyhood chemistry and enable us to protect, love, care and provide for them.

Another indication of our evolved paternalistic instinct is from a recently concluded, 70-year study of the modern Neanderthal, represented by 268 white male Harvard sophomores recruited in the early 1940s. What turned out to be most important in their lives? Relationships. Family. To be needed. Loving and being loved. Despite our macho fantasy, these turn out to be the essence of our manhood.

And contrary to popular belief, the caveman did not club his mate over the head. They really needed each other to survive and more brain research indicates he was likely doing everything he could to score points with the cave mom in his life. Not a lot of evolutionary change there.

*Regardless of whether one believes in evolution, this does refute the claims of many of our mates that we have not engaged in any evolution ourselves.

100 Millennium History of Fatherhood

The recent emergence of the "new, involved, nurturing dad" is actually a re-emergence from way back in caveman time. So how did fathers do in the 100,000 year interim since cave dads showed us how? Great... until about a century ago.

The Romans wrote about families as the basic building block of humanity; moms, dads and kids bound together by love and commitment to each other. Not only did fathers have a major role in defending and providing for their families, they were together with them for the most part, all day and night, and were instinctively teaching them the ways of life.

On the other side of the world, the Mayans had it figured out too and recognized that not only do parents contribute differently to their baby's care, they compliment each other.

So what happened a century ago? The Industrial Revolution came into full swing, which meant fathers were leaving their homes in small villages and on farms in droves. Henry Ford attracted thousands to Detroit where dad worked 10 hours a day, 6 days a week and mom took care of the house and kids. With dad earning more money for his family, this seemed to be a step up for both.

Fast forward 50 years. This increasing affluence meant nicer homes with dishwashers and vacuums that made life easier for moms, who were socially constrained to homemaking and child rearing. They largely took over (because that was their job), to the point that it was a matter of pride for mothers to roll their eyes at the notion that fathers had a clue as to how to take care of

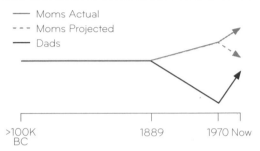

Dad and mom's involvement with children

— Moms Actual
- - - Moms Projected
— Dads

>100K BC   1889   1970 Now

a baby. Fathers embraced this opportunity to avoid dirty diapers and crying babies, and as our hands-on care diminished, our innate dad instincts went into hibernation. We bottomed out in about 1975, and then started our climb back when fathers were allowed to watch their babies being born again.

By now our instincts have re-awakened and we have remembered what we had forgotten. A child can add a great deal to our lives, both the demands and opportunities to protect and care for someone who loves us in return.

That smile we get from our 3-month-old baby (and only our baby can do this to us) sends a surge of oxytocin right through our whole being; we not only light up with a smile ourselves, our brains automatically shift to play time (the default state for a dad) and we pick him up into the air, doing our dad things that help him grow and thrive, and of course generate more smiles.

> " It's OK for dad to have a different way of doing things. Mom might tell you that there's only one way to do it, but you can still do things your way."
>
> — Veteran Dad

We dads are back, we're on a roll, and the more we cut our ancient instincts loose, the more we offer our kids and ourselves. So get your caveman on, it's how you'll benefit your baby most.

Welcome to Fatherhood: We're Here to Help

We Learned To Do It Our Way

In 1990 we started a workshop with fathers and their babies, orienting dads-to-be, and called it Boot Camp for New Dads. We found that dealing with crying babies, crying moms, and the many issues that emerge is a lot easier when you learn what works from dads who have been there and done it.

We wanted to do it our own way, so no women over 2-feet tall were allowed. The dads-to-be returned as experienced fathers along with their own babies to prepare the next group of guys, and this non-profit expanded across the U.S. to England and Canada. Over 300,000 men have joined us to learn how to get a good start as a father.

Along the way, research has found that by following our instincts and doing what comes naturally, we dads help our babies grow in unique and essential ways. Doing so turns out to be a great way to raise a family, as mom gets much-appreciated balance in her life and we and our children also have fun.

Today We Have More Opportunity

Today each successive generation of fathers is enjoying a closer connection with their children, and our sons no doubt will raise the bar further. While we face obstacles to being close to our kids (like long work hours or simply not knowing how), we also are riding a wave of support and encouragement from those around us, especially other dads who show us by example. While our own fathers or grandfathers generally got the short end of the stick, for us, doors are opening, including the ones many of us go through when we leave work early for our child's soccer game.

ADVICE ON ALL THAT ADVICE

If you listen to the "experts," many whom conflict with one another, you'll think that you need a Ph.D. in infant development to take your baby home. And then there are the multitudes, ranging from your mother-in-law to strangers on the streets, who want to tell you whether you will be having a boy or girl, the kinds of foods mom should be eating or how to create a baby genius by 3 months.

Take all "advice" with a grain of salt; ultimately, you and your mate will decide what is best for your family.

> " Sometimes the Rookies will talk about something they've read and the Vets will say, 'Well, that sounds good, but here's what really happens.'"
> — Veteran Dad

We Also Have
More Responsibility

We are delivering on our commitment to do our best for our kids, and it is a lot of work. In fact, it is three times the amount of time our fathers put in. Fatherhood has gotten tougher and no matter your circumstances, at some point you will be seriously challenged. Many of you will exhibit a depth of strength and courage you had no idea was inside you. You will be surprised how much of it comes naturally, though you shouldn't be, since for several millennia (until the 1800's industrial revolution) we all worked out of our homes. Recent research has also found that this ancestry equipped us with biological capabilities that enable us to patiently rock our colicky baby to sleep as well as pull him out of a burning building.

Dads Definitely
Have More Fun

Turns out this is the way it has been for those millennia, and as it is meant to be. Research has found that playing is essential to a baby's full development, and that fathers are babies' natural buddies. Our roughhousing refines their motor skills and confidence, and our inclination to show them the world expands their horizons and teaches them to take risks. The adventure continues with a tour of the hardware store, then some baby wrestling, growing corn with a toddler who loves mud (girls too), fishing with a 2-year-old with a plastic fish on her line, and later sharing a passion for surfing or website development, or perhaps climbing mountains together – whatever your future together brings.

We Can Help You
Do It Your Way

There are many ways to be a great dad, and we are here to help you find the way that works best for you, not tell you how to do it. *Crash Course for Dads-To-Be* summarizes what we have learned from the many thousands of men who have participated in Boot Camp for New Dads workshops; it is what you need to know to get a great start as a father. Check out DadsAdventure.com for more in-depth information on any issue that concerns you.

We are here to help your do you best as a dad and make fatherhood the adventure of your life. Good luck, and consider us your brothers-(with babies)-in-arms.

> " From the moment we went public that my wife was pregnant, the advice poured in. People with kids: 'You get barfed on a lot.'; people without kids: 'Dude, I hear they go through 20 diapers a day. That's like a diaper an hour.'; people with multiple kids: 'Oh, one is nothing. Wait 'til number 4...'; people with grandkids: 'I hope this one cries as much as you did.'; type-A people: 'You must get this book. Don't read that book, it's totally wrong.'; type-B people: Get ready to get barfed on, a lot.'; negative people: 'Kiss your life goodbye.'; positive people: 'You'll be awesome. It probably won't even matter that you get barfed on, a lot.' "
>
> — Veteran Dad

Issues to Not Worry About;
A Few to Plan On

We would like to say "no worries, mate," but the reality is that a man becoming a father has a lot on his mind. Our collective experience and suggestions can help you sort through your issues and get on a constructive track:

Don't Worry About...
...Taking Care of Your Baby

Many men are concerned about taking care of crying babies, changing dirty diapers, etc. In our workshops, even the most nervous guy takes only a few minutes to get used to holding a baby. After just three times changing, feeding, burping or bathing their own baby, they have it down. While the first days can be harrowing, you will get 80% of it down after two weeks and be an expert on your own baby after four. Check out our baby care tips in *Chapter 3* and watch videos of real dads taking care of their babies at DadsAdventure.com. You'll quickly realize that you can too.

...Your Baby's Birth

Go ahead and worry about your baby — everyone does. And worrying about your wife being in pain is standard as well. To minimize any concerns about your ability to help her through as her birth coach, we put everything you need to know in the *Childbirth Coaching Guide*. Tear it out and put it in your hospital bag and you'll do fine.

Think About ...
...The New Mom in Your Life

Some new fathers are stunned by a rapid decline in their relationships once the baby arrives; others find theirs flourishing. If you understand how a wife transforms into a mother, and how to support her, work together raising your baby and bring back the romance, yours will flourish. See *Caring for a New Mom on page 60* for what you need to know.

...The Economics of a Baby

Your family's finances will change and you'll need to respond constructively. In addition to balancing the new family budget, this includes deciding who works, who cares for the baby, commitments to long commutes or big mortgages, how both you and mom can bring balance to your lives, etc. Big changes may be in order; see *Strategies For When Your Time is Short on page 84, Involvement & Balance on page 86* and *Preparing for Your Family's Future on page 114* for tips.

> " Everybody says it's going to change your life. OK - well, what does that mean?"
>
> — Veteran Dad

Expect...
...Ambivalence at Times

Expect downs with the ups; you may cry joyfully at her birth and wonder what you got yourself into a week later. This is surprising and runs counter to your expectations, but sleep deprivation, rapid change in your life and the sacrifices you make can overwhelm your feelings for a child you barely know.

...To Gain Strength from Your Baby

A child can bring out the best in us and can make us stronger. All of us have issues we would like to handle — from getting a degree to quitting smoking — and when we hold our very immortality in our arms and he smiles at us, motivation to get it done comes easier. The fulfillment you get from being a dad will fuel your drive to do more.

...It to Go Fast

A baby comes out in a rapidly evolving state; this means that if you are not engaged or around, you will miss out and may live to regret it. The worst parts also pass quickly – crying due to colic is generally over by 3 months – although it seems a lot longer.

... To Come Last for a While

The most distinguishing characteristic of a man who transforms into a dad is that he is no longer self-centered – his priorities shift to his child, mom, work and then himself. Tougher for some than others. Do a status check on your priorities occasionally to see how you are doing. (See *A New Father's Transformation Milestones* on page 93).

Plan to Be Proactive

It is easy to just get swept along in mom's wake on the changes a new baby brings, but you run the risk of being swept in a direction you will regret. Fatherhood is a huge rite of passage for any man, and getting educated, developing a plan and getting involved is a no-brainer. A good place to start? Ask yourself what your own father was like and how you want to be.

UNCONDITIONAL LOVE

Billionaire Warren Buffet, 83, is worth about $50 billion. When asked what made him what he is today, he said it was the unconditional love he received from his father. "I knew I could always come back home. There is no power on earth like unconditional love. And I think that if you offered that to your child, I mean, you're 90 per-cent of the way home. There may be days when you don't feel like it – it's not uncritical love; that's a different animal – but to know you can always come back, that is huge in life. That takes you a long, long way. And I would say that every parent out there that can extend that to their child at an early age, it's going to make for a better human being."

Connect with Your Baby Before Birth

A mother's bond to her baby is hard-wired. We fathers have to build ours from scratch, and we can start early by doing simple things that make him real in our own minds, and enable our natural feelings for our child to surface and grow.

Track His Amazing Transformation

The egg transforms into a little tadpole that grows arms and legs and then a heart that starts beating. Amazing stuff, and if you track these changes, when he arrives, you'll feel like you already know him.

Listen to Her Heartbeat

Go with mom to her doctor visits. You'll be able to hear your baby's heartbeat at 3 to 4 months with a stethoscope and even earlier with an ultrasound device. It's amazing to actually hear her and listen to a real heartbeat that sounds strong and even powerful for how small she is.

> " I sang the same song to him three times a day. When the cesarean was done and he was on the warmer by himself, I was able to console him by singing that same tune. He knew who I was immediately. And familiarity seemed to calm him down."
>
> — Veteran Dad

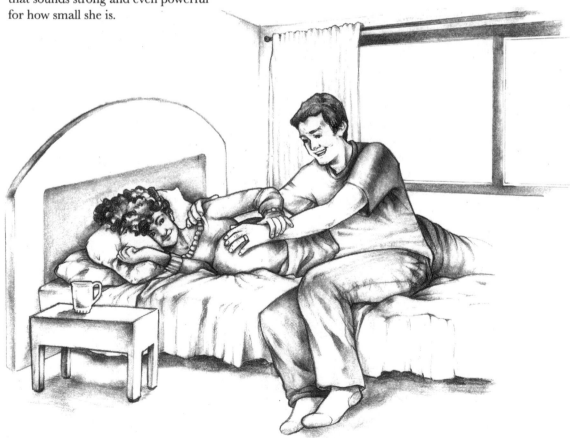

See Him in a Sonogram

It's a big moment for us guys when we see him for the first time. He's all there and this picture is worth a lot more than words. Get one for your wallet. If you're lucky you might see him move.

Feel Her Kick

Around 6 months, when mom invites you to put your hand on her tummy, you'll feel your baby move for the first time. Whoa, she 's really in there! Later on you'll be shocked by how hard your baby can kick. Spooning in bed with mom is a great way to feel her.

Talk to Him, Give Him a Nickname

If you make a habit of talking to him in mom's belly, your baby will recognize your voice when you first talk to him after he's born. As he hears and sees you for the first time, he seems to know you are his father. It's a magical moment for you and a real comfort for him in his strange new world.

Imagine What You Will Do Together

If you think about the adventures you want to have together, whether it's teaching her to fish, surf, work on cars or name the stars, you are not only more likely to do these things, but it is a great way to bond as you realize how much you have to look forward to with your child.

Buy or Build Something for Her

Go out by yourself and pick something meaningful, like her first baseball mitt. If you like working with your hands, you might want to refinish a cradle, or build her a sled, toy box, rocking horse, etc. One guy made up a "diaper bag" using a tool bag. His message: "I am changing her diapers, but as soon as she's out, we're working on stuff together" (a surfing or fishing bag can work, golf bags not so much).

Write Down Thoughts About Her

Our children love to hear about the great times we had with them growing up, and we forget much more than we ever remember. Even if you do not write much, record your early thoughts about her as you experience the above events (it helps make it real for you as well).

> " I would read to the baby every night when he was in the belly and sometimes he would be kicking and as soon as I held him and introduced myself ("I'm your dad"), he stopped crying and looked straight at me. It was out of this world – awesome – an out of body experience. To see him calm down and have that memory – it's surreal. You can explain it all you want but when it happens – whoa. It's like a big gaping hole was in you and he just filled it up."
>
> — Veteran Dad

To-Do Lists Before Birth

For the Hospital
☐ Pre-register.
☐ Clarify what is an isn't covered by your health insurance so you know what out-of-pocket costs you'll have or limitations to your coverage.
☐ Find out where to park and enter the hospital.
☐ Tour the maternity ward; ask a lot of questions.
☐ Help your wife prepare a birth plan. (See sample at birthplan.com).
☐ Keep the car maintained with a full tank of gas.
☐ Make a practice run to the hospital.
☐ Install the car seat.

> Get as much done ahead of time as possible. A big mistake we made was not buying the mini-van before the baby was born. I tell you, going around on weekends with a newborn and talking to salesmen - it's something you really don't want to go through. Get things done early so you can spend more time with your baby."
>
> — Veteran Dad

In the house
☐ Try and get unfinished projects handled prior to junior's arrival.
☐ Check for loose railings, traction on outside steps, clutter in hallways, or other safety hazards for a parent carrying a baby.
☐ Help your wife set up the nursery or area where your baby will sleep.
☐ Stockpile diapers, wipes, clothes, etc.
☐ Obtain other baby equipment and supplies.
☐ Clean bottles and other feeding supplies.
☐ Stock up on batteries (baby toys need them).
☐ Pre-arrange pet care, if needed.

In General
☐ Complete a will or living trust, and consider purchasing life insurance.
☐ Take a class on newborn care, Boot Camp for New Dads, First Aid/CPR, etc.
☐ Put the doctor, hospital, and any other important contact numbers in your cell phone.
☐ Work out general "help" and visit policies for in-laws and friends. (See *Getting Settled at Home on page 21*).
☐ Pack for the hospital in advance, baby could be early.
☐ Make a list of everyone you want to send baby announcements.
☐ Register at a baby store or department store so people will be able to get you what you want.
☐ Register with websites, such as babycenter.com and you'll not only get great information, you'll also get coupons and discounts on baby stuff.
☐ Get your baby a Social Security number, either at the hospital, when filling out information for the birth certificate or online at www.ssa.gov.
☐ Enjoy as much time with your wife as you can. It might be a while before you get time alone.

Preparing Yourself

Becoming a father is a process with ups and downs, and the trick is to get ahead of the curve with a pro-active, constructive approach to the challenges you encounter. Holding and caring for a baby before yours arrives goes a long way. Take advantage of opportunities with babies of friends or relatives, or go visit a new father you know and ask him to show you how he does it. See *Transforming Into A Dad* for additional information that will help you prepare.

Nursery Safety

❑ Be careful with used baby equipment. In some cases these items are unsafe, both because of changing safety guidelines and defects from use (such as missing parts).

❑ The Juvenile Products Manufacturers Association (JPMA) sponsors a safety-certification program; check for its seal.

❑ For information on recalled products, visit the U.S. Consumer Product Safety Commission's website at cpsc.gov

❑ Blinds with long pull-cords are a hazard, especially looped cords, as a baby can get these wrapped around her neck. Cut them to prevent an accident.

Arrange Time Off Work

If taking weeks of unpaid leave is not an option, consider the following alternatives:

❑ Working half days to stretch out time off.

❑ Take off one midweek day each week for one to two months, which gives you time with your new child and gives mom a break she can plan on over a period of time.

❑ Ask other recent dads, particularly fellow employees, for their insights and suggestions.

❑ Ask your HR department or manager about other benefits your company might have.

❑ Check out your state laws for any other options that might be open to you.

Negotiating with Your Employer

❑ Try working overtime now in exchange for time off when the baby arrives.

❑ Talk to your boss in advance about using accrued vacation time.

❑ Check out your state laws and union benefits.

> At the beginning of the book, there's a really good pull out and it has a lot of great information in there. The childbirth coaching guide, role of the birth coach, things that are going to be happening and a section at the bottom on what you need to know and need to do. There's a lot of really good, important information and you should stick it in your bag for the hospital right now."
>
> – Veteran Dad

Essential Checklists

Install the Car Seat Early

Install it early and get used to adjusting the straps. National Highway Traffic and Safety Administration recommendations about car-ride safety for your baby are as follows:

1. Use rear-facing convertible or infant-only seat for the first year.
2. Tightly install child seat in car's rear seat, facing the rear (base should not move more than 1 inch).
3. Never use a car seat in a vehicle's front seat that has an air bag.
4. Child seat should recline at approximately a 45-degree angle.
5. Harness strap slots should be at or below the infant's shoulder level. Keep harness straps snug.
6. Place chest clip at infant's armpit level to keep straps in place.
7. If necessary for support, place a rolled towel around your baby's head.

If you need help to get it right, consult seatcheck.org to locate a certified car seat fitting expert near you.

Recommended Baby Items

As you settle in with your baby, sort out what you have and what you still need. These are sure bets according to Boot Camp veterans:

- ❑ Diaper Genie – helps eliminate smells.
- ❑ Bouncy seat (with sound and lights) – entertainment and exercise.
- ❑ Swing – puts your baby to sleep.
- ❑ Soft chest carrier — feels great, keeps him entertained and can put him to sleep.
- ❑ Battery operated stick-on touch lights – convenient and not too bright for a baby or sleeping spouse.
- ❑ Camera and/or video camera.
- ❑ Bassinet or cradle – a small moveable alternative to the crib.
- ❑ Baby bath tub with insert for newborns.
- ❑ Stash of diapers, wipes, and ointments.
- ❑ Bathrobe for mom – a nice big, soft one that she will want to wear for weeks.
- ❑ Big screen TV – you're staying home more.

LIST THINGS YOU LIKE TO DO TOGETHER NOW

As an investment in your relationship, sit down with your wife and make a list of the things you like to do now, before the baby arrives. After life with the baby settles down, pull out the list and pick out something to do. Even if your options are still limited, it will remind you both what you had together, and will make it more likely you will get most of it back.

Final Check List

- ❑ Keep your cell phone charged so you can be contacted anytime during the day.
- ❑ Make arrangements with your work in terms of time off, transitioning workload or possibly designating someone to cover your load. If it is possible, avoid traveling.
- ❑ Have a watch with a second hand or stopwatch/contraction app on your phone to count contractions.
- ❑ Are you ready for the birth? Review the coaching guide to learn the basics.
- ❑ Once the baby is born, put a message on your voice mail announcing the baby's name, size, time of birth, eye color, etc. Ask callers to leave a message and understand that you are busy and it may be a while before you get back to them.

- ❑ _____
- ❑ _____
- ❑ _____

What You Need for the Hospital

Get a list together of the items you need for your hospital bag and make sure mom's and your baby's bags include the basics. Keep the list with your bag to double check before you head out (if you have time). You can get ideas from the hospital staff and birthing classes or talk to someone who recently delivered. Our basic lists include:

Dad's List to Bring

- ❑ Folder of important documents – insurance cards, birth plan (two or three copies), pre-admission forms, etc.
- ❑ Baby book (many nurseries will put your baby's footprint in the book).
- ❑ Watch with second hand or digital readout or contraction/stop watch app on your phone.
- ❑ Change of clothes and pajamas if you are staying overnight.
- ❑ Toiletries: toothbrush, razor, shampoo, deodorant.
- ❑ Comfortable shoes — you may do a lot of walking.
- ❑ CD, iPod or player with her favorite music.
- ❑ Pain-easing tools recommended at birthing classes – tennis balls, hot or cold packs, massagers, lotion, etc.

> " They say women become mothers when they see the blue strip, men become fathers in the delivery room. But I've talked to guys who take a while to actually feel like a father. So, if you're in shock at first, or you don't feel that fatherly instinct for a few days, or even months, give it time and it will kick in."
>
> – Veteran Dad

- ☐ Something to read to mom.
- ☐ Bathing suit for you — help mom take a shower to ease labor pains.
- ☐ Long-sleeve shirt or sweatshirt — Hospitals can be cold.
- ☐ Food and drink in a small cooler: sandwich, power bars and juice, snacks for mom and you after the birth.
- ☐ Cash to have on hand.
- ☐ Pen and pad of paper.
- ☐ Headache medication.
- ☐ Camera with memory card, battery, etc.
- ☐ Address book/phone numbers to announce the birth.
- ☐ Cell phone and charger, or calling card in case you can't use a cell phone in the hospital.
- ☐ Champagne — put your name on it, and ask a nurse to store it in the fridge.
- ☐ Childbirth Coaching Guide at the front of this book.

Basics for Her

- ☐ Nightgown and slippers.
- ☐ Her pillow.
- ☐ Socks to keep her feet warm.
- ☐ Hard candies or suckers.
- ☐ Extra magazines.
- ☐ Infant care reference book.
- ☐ Breast feeding guide book.
- ☐ Glasses/contacts and supplies.
- ☐ Outfit for going home.
- ☐ Makeup and hair care.

Basics for Your Baby

- ☐ Outfit for going home (in style).
- ☐ Hat and booties to keep her warm.
- ☐ Mittens so he does not scratch his face.
- ☐ Two or three receiving blankets for swaddling, etc.
- ☐ Diapers (for newborns) and wipes.
- ☐ If necessary, formula and bottles.

> " Think of it in boxing terms. You're in your wife's corner during the actual birth part of it. You have your birthing plan, and this is the way you want it to go and then of course, there's the way it's going to go. Sometimes it's a little different, sometimes it's completely different. You have to listen to your wife and what she wants, but there's a point where she's in so much pain, or loopey and you have to guide the nurses and doctors. Don't let them completely take over. If you have a plan, or want things to go a certain way, make yourself known and make sure she's ok. You're there for her, not for family, not for anybody else. If you're there making sure she's ok, you're going to be fine."
>
> — New Father

Handling an Emergency Birth

The chances of an emergency birth are extremely small, but it's normal to think about the possibility.

When It's Too Late

If you can see the baby's head (or other part) at the vaginal opening, your mate says she can feel the baby coming, or she can't stop pushing.

Call 911

If you're home alone, call someone to assist and call her doctor. If you're in the car, pull over, put on your flashers. Keep 911 on the line for instructions.

Grab a Blanket

Blankets, clothing, towels, your shirt – something you can wrap the baby in after he is born. Grab two just in case.

Calm Mom and Slow Things Down

Reassure her, tell her that everything's fine. Help her breathe through the contractions instead of pushing.

Get Mom in Position

Get her into a comfortable position lying down. Babies come out fast and are slippery, so be ready. Put something soft under mom where the baby may land.

Get Positioned to Catch Baby

Try to get your partner to stop pushing and to just breathe. As the head appears, let it come out on its own; do not pull.

> " Feeling helpless is one of my worst fears. Not knowing what to do when something unexpected happens."
>
> —Rookie Dad

Check the Umbilical Cord

If the cord is around your baby's neck, carefully slide it over her head.

Clear Your Baby's Airway

Make sure the baby's nose and mouth are clear of mucous that might impede breathing.

Time for the Rest of Him

Encourage mom to start pushing and let him slide out, putting one hand under his head and back and using the other to firmly grasp his feet as he is slippery.

He Should Start Crying

If he doesn't start crying and breathing right away, rub his chest briskly or slap the soles of his feet. If that does not get him breathing, ask for instructions from 911 personnel.

Don't Cut the Cord

It won't hurt anything to leave it until the paramedics arrive or you can get to a hospital.

Place Your Baby on Mom

Wipe the baby off and place her on mom's abdomen on the baby's stomach or side. Cover the baby but make sure you can see her face. Keep your baby and mom warm.

Start the Baby Nursing

If the cord will reach, place the baby at your partner's breast and let him start suckling or nuzzling. This will help reassure mom her baby is fine.

Wait for the Paramedics

If they aren't available, carefully drive to the hospital's emergency entrance. Do not get excited and rush.

CHAPTER 2

Settling In With Your Baby

" One thing
I've learned about
having a kid is,
if you like having
things scheduled,
don't have one."
— Veteran Dad

Make the Most of Your First Day as a Father

Your baby is brand new, your wife is now a new mom, and you are a new father. This is a very special time for you to get to know each other and bond as a family, so relish the moments by just being together, alone. Don't let work or other issues intrude on your first days, and take advantage of the opportunity to care for your baby.

Learn from the Nurses

OB nurses are experts on newborns and are usually happy to teach you basic skills on comforting, changing, bathing and swaddling your baby. They love babies and will be very pleased to know "their baby" has a father who wants to take great care of him. Don't be shy about asking the nurse to show you how, and take advantage of any chance to learn.

Take Care of Mom

Help mom deal with her medical issues, breastfeeding, etc., so you won't be clueless when you get home. Tell her what a great mom she is and how much you love her. Don't let mom feel compelled to have the baby in the room all the time. If she needs a break, ask the nurse if the baby can go to the nursery.

Manage Your Visitors

A few low key visits are cool, and give you a chance to show off the baby, but don't feel pressured to have a lot of visits. The best excuse for limiting visits is: "she is exhausted and needs to sleep," which is generally the case anyway, and visitors can always come by the house later to see the baby. Make sure all visitors wash their hands before handling the baby, as his immune system is underdeveloped. Wash yours, too.

Change Baby's First Diaper

One veteran dad reported that he made it a point to change his baby's first diaper so he "could set the tone" that he was serious about taking care of his child. Then he showed his wife how, which built her confidence in him.

BEFORE YOU LEAVE THE HOSPITAL

- ☐ Get more pictures and get in the picture yourself.
- ☐ Make sure your home is ready; ask for help cleaning, setting the thermostat, stocking it with supplies, etc.
- ☐ Make sure the car is ready with installed baby seat.

Start Falling in Love

"Bonding" is falling in love with your baby. You might fall head over heals the moment you see him. Many dads, however, report feeling disconnected from their child even months after the birth, so if you don't feel "bonded" to your baby at first, don't worry. Becoming a father is a process and you can't rush it. Just take advantage of the opportunities you have to be with him. Hold him in your arms and look in his eyes, check out his fingers and toes, snuggle her to your chest until she falls asleep and feels like she is part of you. If you're feeling uncomfortable, the last thing you want to do is shy away. Just give it time; trust that it will happen.

Welcome to Fatherhood! Try and get some sleep; you're going to need it.

Helping Mom Breastfeed

The broad benefits of breastfeeding have been firmly established by research and a record proportion of mothers (about 75%) are giving it their best shot. Despite a broad assumption that breastfeeding is the most natural (next to birth) thing for a mother to do, many run into problems and quit early. Being natural and being easy are two completely different things, and this means dad has a major support role in helping mom and baby get breastfeeding down.

Common Problems

There are a lot of things that can create problems for your little one when he's trying to eat in those first days:

Latching on: The most common problem for a newborn is latching on properly. There are a variety of positions that can be tried (ask the nurse while you're still in the hospital) to help him get on and stay on.

Nothing coming: For the first few days after the baby is born, mom will only be producing colostrum (a nutritive rich liquid that boosts his immune system) and you might worry he's

not eating enough. Almost every baby loses weight in the first few days, and once mom's milk comes in the weight will come right back.

Pulling off: Maybe she can latch on, but after just a couple of minutes she pulls off. This gets better in time as she slowly learns to coordinate sucking, drinking, and breathing.

> " If I could tell you one thing ... encourage your partner to breastfeed for as long as possible. Formula is expensive!"
>
> — Veteran Dad

It takes most babies a few weeks to get breastfeeding down completely. By the third week just about every baby can breastfeed with no trouble, and those early problems will largely be a part of the past.

How Dad Can Help

If mom and baby are having a difficult time with breastfeeding there are things you can do to help:

Help mom relax: This can be anything from a shoulder rub to the tried and true bringing her a glass of water or something to eat while she's nursing. When she's relaxed, the milk will let down. An engineer in Boot Camp for New Dads had a good check list for problem solving breastfeeding: Mom relaxed?

Milk letting down? Baby getting enough? Baby calm enough to suck? Well positioned?

Get covered: Read up on what your insurance coverage is for breast pumps and supplies. Breastfeeding supplies are tax deductible, so use that flexible spending account to pay for them.

Burp the baby: Before mom switches breasts, take the baby and burp him. This will give mom a short break, and allows you to be a part of feeding.

Calm the baby: If she's having a hard time feeding and is getting upset, take the baby and calm her down, that way both mom and baby get a little down time before trying again.

After three weeks, pitch in: Suggest that mom pump her breast milk so you can get in on the feeding and she can get a break.

Get More Help if Needed

Most hospitals offer lactation classes or you can often have a lactation nurse visit while you're still in the hospital, so take full advantage. Mom can face problems such as medications that preclude breastfeeding, inadequate milk production, poor letdown, inverted nipples that a baby can't latch on to, or finding breastfeeding to be too painful or demanding, especially if she feels pressure to return to work quickly. If so, suggest she talk with the lactation consultant to be sure she is aware of all alternatives. Use of a breast pump may work, in which case your baby gets breast milk and you can get in on the feeding. If problems persist, you can get help from a certified breastfeeding counselor through La Leche League at www.llli.org or the International Lactation Consultant Association at www.ilca.org. Find more advice at breastmilk.com, babycenter.com/breastfeeding or by calling the Breastfeeding Helpline at 1-800-994-9662.

IF IT JUST WON'T WORK

Given all the benefits, it is tough for moms to stop breastfeeding even when it is not going to work. Your job is to reassure her of your love and respect. New mothers tend to beat themselves up over this, and your partner will need your support now more than ever. Even if you are disappointed that your baby will not be breast fed, the bottom line is helping your mate overcome her disappointment and getting on with becoming the best mom possible to your child.

Getting Settled at Home

The exciting, exhausting 24/7 days of parenting a newborn really kick in as you drive away from the supportive embrace of the hospital. With your wife and infant in the back seat, you head off into an adventure that will require the supply lines, equipment, logistics, communications and support troops of a small military operation. It may as well be a covert gig as you will be going deep under cover and won't resurface for two to three months.

Arrange a Support System

Arrange for help from family, friends, and professionals (e.g., visiting nurse) if needed. It's a good idea to keep a list handy with phone numbers and other contact information. (See *page 25*). Don't expect your wife to handle arrangements if she usually does; she will be focused on the baby. After a C-section, plan on handling everything for two weeks.

Make a list of who you and mom want to ask for help, and then ask. Don't be shy about saying no to offers from those who will add rather than relieve stress. If you have family nearby, your baby will be the focus of attention for the first few weeks, so put them to work. Out-of-town relatives do not need to stay with you 24/7.

> As far as in-laws, you want them to relieve stress, not add to it. So you need to figure out - are they the type to help you take care of things around the house? That first month, it's hard to keep the house up, so if they're really helpful in the sense of doing housework, definitely have them. But, you still need to be on your guard to make sure your wife isn't stressing out about having guests."
>
> — Veteran Dad

Keep Help Helpful

The right help makes a huge difference. Some "help" can be intrusive; working out a policy can keep everyone happy and involved:

- Use a calendar page (see *page 26*) to schedule help, visitors, meal deliveries, and doctor visits for at least the first two weeks.
- Post a "to do" list on a dry-erase board where you can note what needs to be done, so no one has to ask.
- Grandma is there to help, not hog the baby. Deal with it by asking her to show you what she knows.
- Even just a few days will be appreciated by you and mom, but too much can be a problem.
- You may not need as much help as you planned on, or may need more due to postpartum depression, colicky baby, etc.
- No drama, criticisms of mom, competition for the baby, etc., allowed. Make mom's life easier.
- If you can afford it, hire a house cleaner, get a baby sitter, bring in a doula, etc.

FIRST LINE OF DEFENSE

Set your voicemail message to announce the baby's name, weight, height, date and time of birth, and let callers know you will get back to them when you can. Turn cell phones off when napping.

Get Organized/Get Efficient

The trick is to settle into a manageable routine that you can maintain once the help leaves. To make it easier:

- Set up a breastfeeding station with a rocker, reading material, TV remote and phone or tablet charger.
- Stock up on quick meals, take your friends up on offers to bring meals, use online grocery shopping and restaurant delivery; make large amounts of soups and stews and freeze the extra.
- Use disposable plates and utensils for the first two weeks.
- Keep a diaper bag stocked with baby items to facilitate fast getaways when the need or opportunity arises.
- Rather than sleepers with lots of snaps, dress your baby in gowns to make night changes easier.
- Put mini-changing station baskets with diapers, wipes, lotion and a toy in strategic locations around the house.
- Ramp up your home entertainment system with money saved staying home, and arrange access to music, movies, etc.
- Get creative and devise your own solutions to issues that emerge during the first two to three weeks.

❝ When you first get home, you've got to be in that protector role. You're kind of like the gatekeeper of the house. Eveyone's going to want to come and visit and see the baby, and that's all well and good, but you and your wife probably need to talk and establish what the guidelines are."

— Veteran Dad

VISITATION GROUND RULES

Balance loved ones wanting to see your baby with your new family's needs. Together, set some ground rules for visitors:

- No unannounced or marathon visits.
- No waking up the baby.
- Mom can't take care of guests.
- Visitors must wash hands before touching the baby.
- Don't handle the baby too much.
- No sick visitors, especially children.
- No unsolicited opinions.
- Diapers/meals required to enter.
- Help with housework is encouraged.

Enforcing the rules is dad's job (Some guys have to tell their mother-in-law, or even their own mother, to back off).

Strategies for Surviving the First Weeks

Make Sleep a Priority

Fatigue is typically the first and toughest challenge faced by new parents, especially nursing moms. Babies start with six to eight sleep/awake cycles per day compared to our one. Even if you have been exhausted before, it probably won't be like this. Sleep deprivation can cause irritability and even disorientation and a vicious cycle can develop in which you cannot relax and go to sleep even when you have time. Make sleep a priority when you arrive home:

- **Provide opportunities for your partner to sleep** several hours during the day by taking full charge of the baby between certain breastfeedings. If necessary, insist she do so; many new mothers feel compelled to do more than they need to.
- **Trade shifts with mom** so you can sleep. Grab a nap when your baby is sleeping on your watch; put him safely on your chest where he will make sure you remember that you are on first call.
- **Stock up on sleep when relatives are around** to take shifts, or arrange a baby sitter for several hours.
- Work out an arrangement for night in which you can **share the load** most efficiently (i.e., you both don't need to get up every time the baby wakes up). Talk

> On getting to sleep your self ... naps are good. Deep coma sleep is gone for now."
> — Veteran Dad

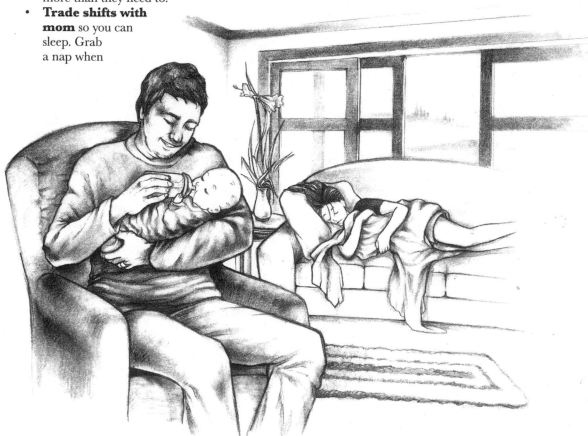

to other parents about ideas and try out your own; e.g., a co-sleeper can make night breast feedings much easier on mom as she doesn't have to fully wake up, making it easier to get back to sleep.

- **Start out building good baby sleep habits** (see *How Can I Help My Baby Go to Sleep? on page 38*), and don't get hung up with the debate over letting babies cry it out – there is a pragmatic middle ground to choose as well.

Get a Grip on Colic

For healthy babies, colic presents new parents' worst scenario. Incessant crying, less sleep, anger at your baby, feelings of failure and antagonism between mom and dad can combine to make your lives miserable for three months. You need to get ahead of the curve by becoming the expert on the aggressive crying mitigation techniques found in *Troubleshooter's Guide To Crying Babies page 40*, on DadsAdventure.com and in *The Happiest Baby on the Block* video.

" The first two weeks – the main thing we did was make sure we didn't have people coming by because you have to find your rhythm. We actually had her mom come and stay with us. We weren't entertaining her or taking care of her. She was there to do laundry and the dishes. You gotta be selfish. You gotta find your own system."

— Veteran Dad

" If it's not critical and doesn't have to be done, then I'm sleeping. It was hard to get her there too, but she finally got there. But I still have to remind her."

— Veteran Dad

Blow off Non-Essential Tasks

Minimize outside work responsibilities so you can concentrate on your new family. Prioritize essential tasks and focus on the basics:

- Feeding, changing and caring for your newborn.
- Eating, sleeping and showering yourselves.
- Getting to know your baby; he'll be a newborn for only a few short weeks.

Make sure any dishes are washed and the trash taken out so clutter does not add to the stress. If you cannot assign tasks to help, cut back on routine ones like cooking, laundry, shopping, vacuuming, and errand-running during the first weeks. You can catch up later. Set aside everything else like thank-you notes.

Lighten up on your expectations and encourage mom to do the same. During these initial weeks, perfectionism regarding housework is a vice, not a virtue. Be flexible and go with the flow, and after a week or so, your new life with a baby will start settling into a regular routine.

Form a Parenting Team

Nothing is more important than you and your mate working together. Learn to take care of your baby together at first, and then take shifts to give each other a break and make the best use of your time. If mom insists on doing it all, suggest she back off for her own good. Stick together no matter what. Building a family is a profound responsibility for you two.

Support & Emergency Contacts

Emergency number 911	Poison Center 1-800-222-1222
Hospital emergency room	Nurse answer line
Baby's pediatrician	Mom's obstetrician
Lactation consultant	
Friend	Friend
Relative	Relative
Dad Contact	Mom Contact
Nanny or day care center	Alarm Company
Plumber	Veterinarian
Dentist	Take-out restaurant
Other	Other

Child's Information

First Name	Last Name
Date of Birth	Hair/Eye color
Weight	as of (date)
Medical Conditions	Allergies
Health Insurance	Policy/Group #

Weekly Survival Chart

	Sunday	Monday	Tuesday	Wednesday	Thursday	Friday	Saturday
Morning — BREAKFAST							
Morning — SUPPORT							
Morning — TO DO							
Afternoon — LUNCH							
Afternoon — SUPPORT							
Afternoon — TO DO							
Night — DINNER							
Night — SUPPORT							
Night — TO DO							

Note who brings dinner, when basic household tasks are to be done, doctor visits, who is coming to help, etc. A plan makes it less overwhelming

Strategies for Thriving in the First Weeks

Don't Miss This Opportunity to Bond as a New Family

Having family help out can be great when you and mom are exhausted, but the first few weeks with a new baby are also a time for a new dad, mom and baby to get to know each other. Spend time alone, just the three of you. You and mom will get to know the baby's habits and routines, and you'll feel comfortable as parents more quickly.

Take Great Care of Mom

This is the first piece of advice new fathers tell dads-to-be. Their specific advice includes:

- Tell her what a great mother she is. Reassure her about any concerns she has. Tell her you love her.
- Protect her from intrusive visitors, help her maximize sleep, and make sure she eats well with regular meals.
- Understand her "ownership" issues regarding the baby. Be patient.
- Help her get a daily bath or shower, out of her robe, and some exercise.
- Get her time on her own to read, take a bath or listen to music.
- Give her more time out of the house so she can take a walk, visit a friend, go to an exercise class, or just breathe.
- Make sure she gets appropriate health care and help her with any "baby blues" or depression issues. See *Baby Blues & Postpartum Depression on page 64.*
- Encourage her to join and regularly participate in a local mothers group so she does not feel isolated.

Additional tips can be found in *How To Support A Mom-To-Be on page 54.*

> " Make sure that you have time for just you three. Because everybody wants to come and see the baby. You've just started this family, so you want to make sure you have that bonding time."
>
> — Veteran Dad

Romance and Fun

Well, not much romance at first, but it is never too early to start warming her back up. Getting out and making her laugh is a great way to start. Newborns sleep for hours and can be quiet enough to allow you to go to a restaurant or movie. Just getting out together to take the baby for a walk in the stroller can invigorate your bond. See *Romancing a New Mom on page 66.*

Your Attitude Counts Big

In the first weeks after the birth, new moms often find themselves on an emotional roller coaster with feelings ranging from deep happiness to inadequacy and frustration. Dads are usually along for the ride. As time wears on, new moms and dads wear down, and start asking "will it ever end?" It's a prescription for turning "starting a family" into a depressing experience.

When the chips are down, attitude means everything, and with mom focused on the baby, this mostly means your attitude. We'll spare you the platitudes (e.g., suck it up) because you won't want to hear them, but just know that this is your trial by fire on your path to fatherhood. Consider the following to help maintain your attitude:

- Boost or reactivate your's and mom's sense of humor by stocking up on your favorite funny movies or shows.
- Get together with other new parents; sharing experiences is very therapeutic as there is always someone worse off.
- Take care of yourself in terms of health, and get some time alone with your buddies on occasion.
- If things get real tough, knowing that you were there when your child really needed you will last a lifetime.

Make Your Fatherhood Your Own

As a new dad today, you have unprecedented opportunities to be part of your child's life. You also have forces pushing you away, such as your career commitments, your current life that you know and love, or perhaps mom's gate keeping or the example set by your own father. You have serious choices to make.

The counter force comes from your child, who is designed to compete effectively for your heart. The trick for you is to trust yourself with your baby, spend time together away from mom, and follow your instincts. Dads tend to be creative problem solvers, so if baby is fussy, come up with your own solution like holding him and bouncing on an exercise ball. Buy matching hats. Teach him a secret handshake. If you learn to put him to sleep by safely mounting his car seat on an idling large block Chevy V8 engine (the low rumble mimics a mother's heartbeat), you will be a legend among dads, and you will have definitively made your fatherhood your own.

" When you are with the baby in the first few weeks, and go 'Oh – I got the diaper' and you take that step to be more involved, it kind of shows that you are gonna be there – you're gonna be involved. And I think that takes a huge weight off of their shoulders. Because then they can relax and they go 'OK – we're going to make it. We're going to be OK and it's not all just going to be me.' And I think that's a lot of what moms are worried about – that once the baby comes that the father's not going to be around and just going to go off and watch football."

— Veteran Dad

MARRIAGE COUNSELING AND ROMANCE

tiny.cc/MarriageMaintenance
Online support, links and resources.

Counsel-Search.com
Find a Marriage Counselor in your area.

MarriageAdvice.com
Articles on a variety of marriage subjects.

How to Get out of the House

Basic sanity requires that you leave the confines of your house as soon as possible. This will include taking your baby out alone or with mom, taking your wife out on a date alone, and even taking yourself out (for good behavior). Sheer exhaustion in the first weeks should not preclude this, as it is the antidote to the parental stress that develops early on from feeling trapped, closed-in and housebound with an incessantly demanding infant.

Dads need to take the initiative because a new mom is generally just trying to get through the day and may not get out of her bathrobe for two weeks. Don't wait six weeks for his immune system to charge up; just don't go where he will be around other people. Getting out also overcomes the "stuck at home with the baby" inertia that can otherwise set in for years, and sets in motion an active, outgoing family lifestyle.

Progressive Outings

- Pack her in the stroller and take a walk around the block. This works well with crying babies as nobody is bothered and the rumbling ride of the stroller is soothing to her. You may add a side-to-side rocking motion to enhance the effect, or cover the stroller opening with a blanket to turn out the lights (or keep the sun off her face).
- Place her in the soft front carrier facing you and go for a walk or even a short hike. The warmth of your body and walking motion will calm her and lull her to sleep; you get some exercise and relaxation as well. Since she is so close, you can talk or sing to her softly.

- You already put her in the car, strapped in according to specs, for the ride home, so the next step is to develop a proficient routine because you will be doing this a lot. Pack the diaper bag, the stroller, front carrier or later a backpack carrier so you are fully prepared for the adventures ahead.
- Make it a habit. Take her with you regularly, and figure out how to keep to her sleep schedule while out and about. She will remind you of her feeding schedule; just bring the milk, bottle and a portable bottle warmer.

Take Your Baby Out to Eat

Restaurants and fussy babies don't mix, but you can eat out in peace:
- Work around her fussy times; try breakfast when she is rested.
- When waiting for dinner (to prevent fussiness) walk her around and show her pictures in the hall, etc.
- If she gets fussy, wrap her in a blanket and take a walk outside to calm her, or park her next to you in her stroller and rock it side-to-side.
- If it is just not working, ask to have your food to-go and try again another day.

Put Baby to Sleep Anywhere

Maintaining your baby's sleep routine does not mean it must occur in her crib. The schedule is the key, and the stroller, front carrier, and car seat all can work. If eating out during her normal nap time, place her in her seat near the table and rock it with your foot. If you go to a park, a small portable bed can work; try replicating her normal sleeping environment, wrap her up in a familiar blanket from her crib and hold her so she gets warm and falls asleep, or walk her in a stroller. Be creative; there is always a solution.

Challenges Getting Out Alone with Your Baby

Fear. The thought of taking your infant out on your own can be unnerving – until you do it once. Mom may not quite trust you at first, but after a few trips when you bring your baby home safe and sound (no need to report minor problems), there is little she will appreciate more than her time alone and knowing her baby has a great dad.

> " One thing that scores brownie points with moms: Sometime in that first month, you go and take that baby out of the house for a couple hours. Even just an hour. And don't let mom come with you.
>
> "It does a couple of things: One – it gets you stock with mom because you're bringing the baby back and the baby's still alive, so it reassures mom that you can take care of the baby. But also, it gets mom a little bit of time too. Because even if you're still in the house and say "go get some rest," she's still worried if the baby's in the other room.
>
> "So, get out of the house, or kick mom out of the house for a couple of hours. That will help her get confidence in you. Because part of our job is reassuring mom that we can take care of the baby."
>
> – Veteran Dad

CHAPTER 3

Caring For A New Baby

> **"**He cried for an hour and a half straight and I'm thinking, 'Am I a bad Dad? Did I have a bad baby?' But they cry because they're trying to tell you something."
> — Veteran Dad

Learning to Care for Your New Baby

A Little Education and Some On-The-Job Training, and You Will Become an Expert

We learn best by doing, but a little instruction goes a long way. Try the following:

- Learn the techniques below from the nurses in the hospital before you go home.
- Take a class on new baby care. Doing this with your partner allows you to learn as a team.
- Learn from real experts – new fathers of twins – on the Crash Course for Dads-To-Be DVD. Watch it with your wife, and she'll see that men are capable of caring for an infant.
- Check out baby care websites, like babycenter.com; ivillage.com; aap.org; americanbaby.com.

Quick Guide to Brand New Infant Care

This is what you need to know to get started immediately with your baby:

DIAPER CHANGES

1. Put diaper, wipes, cream, clothes, etc., within reach; lay baby on changing pad on a secure surface and keep one hand on him at all times.
2. Talk to him to distract him and minimize any fussing.
3. Undo the diaper; if a boy, place a clean diaper over his tummy and penis to avoid getting peed on.
4. If poopy, grab baby's ankles and lift over his chest and use top of old diaper to wipe away as much as you can and then tuck it under him.
5. Use wipes to thoroughly clean remaining poop. For girls, always wipe front to back to avoid infection.
6. Use diaper cream so the meconium in his first few stools doesn't stick to his bottom like tar. Use it on any rash that develops as well.
7. Put a new, open diaper under his bottom, fasten it snuggly and fold top down below his umbilical cord stump.
8. Put the used wipes in the dirty diaper and roll it up, re-applying the old tape to keep it closed.
9. Wash your hands or use a hand sanitizer.

CORD CARE

Umbilical cord stumps need to be kept clean and dry before they fall off in one to three weeks. Use a cotton swab with rubbing alcohol to clean it two to three times a day while changing diapers.

BATHING

1. For the first weeks, give him a sponge bath to avoid getting his cord stump wet.
2. Put warm water in a bowl, have some mild soap handy, undress him and place him on a towel.
3. Get a soft cloth wet, add a little soap and wipe him down gently starting with his head to his toes. Be thorough on his bottom and any skin creases.
4. Rinse him using another cloth with clean water, dry him off and dress him in a clean outfit.

> " One time my wife left me with our baby, Madison, so she could run some errands. After my wife left, Madison wouldn't stop crying. I panicked and decided to call my wife. Just before I punched in the last number I decided NO, I'm not going to call her. I hung up the phone and started finding ways to calm Madison down. A half-hour later she finally calmed down. It proved to be a real confidence builder for me."
>
> – Veteran Dad

FEEDING (WITH A BOTTLE)

See Helping Mom Breastfeed
1. Sit the baby on your lap and recline her slightly so that she is cradled in one of your arms.
2. Support her head and place the nipple in her mouth.
3. She may not be hungry for the first few days; to help trigger a sucking reflex, rub nipple gently on her lips or the roof of her mouth.
4. If she gags on the formula, pull nipple back a little.
5. Let her eat until she's finished.

BURPING AFTER FEEDING

1. While in a slightly reclined sitting position, take the baby and, while supporting his head, lay him on you chest-to-chest. Use a burp cloth – he may spit up.
2. Support the baby with one arm (under his butt) while gently but firmly patting his back with your free hand.
3. If nothing happens after a few minutes change his position up over your shoulder and try again.
4. If nothing happens, he likely does not need to burp.

SWADDLING

1. Spread a receiving blanket on a flat surface.
2. Place her diagonally on the blanket with her head on one corner.
3. With one hand, bring the bottom corner up to her chin so her legs are tucked in.
4. With the other hand, pull a side corner snuggly over her and tuck it between her back and the blanket.
5. Pull the other corner over her and tuck it in.

MASSAGING

To relax your baby and get him to sleep longer, massage him by stroking him lightly in smooth, circular motions on the head, arms, stomach and legs. You can do it over his clothes or you can use a little baby oil on his skin.

DAD IS 'HERE TO PLAY'

Years ago, a Boot Camp dad-to-be said he was not the most "domesticated" male around, and his relatives and friends, and even his wife expected him to shy away from caring for a baby. He wanted to prove them wrong when it came to his own baby, so he made sure he was the one to change his baby's first diaper. He said that he wanted to set the tone that he was "here to play".

It worked. The joke and subtle criticisms about his attitude and skills regarding babies stopped, and those around him started taking him seriously. They looked up to him as a father who was committed to taking the best possible care of his child. It felt good and he found their respect encouraged him to do even more. Even his wife treated him differently; she was both relieved and proud of him as the father of their child. It feels good to be respected as a father and respect drives us to do our best.

Milestones for New Dads

Fatherhood has changed. Today, the expectations for a dad are much higher, but this also provides more opportunity for your baby to be an important part of your life.

If you like to set goals in order to measure accomplishments, then start with these seven milestones for your first three months as a father. If you're an overachiever, you can always speed up the timetable or add more milestones:

1. Get hands-on experience with your baby from the very beginning at the birth and throughout the hospital stay.
2. Learn the basics of holding, changing, dressing, burping, and swaddling within one week.
3. Learn to comfort your crying baby within two weeks. If he has colic, try not to get too frustrated and make it four weeks.
4. Select one activity – like bathing your baby or giving her "tummy time" to build upper-body strength – and make it your own within four weeks.
5. When he's 6 weeks start going out with your baby, just the two of you; walks, stroller rides, etc. Get out at least once a week.
6. Spend four hours alone with your baby by the end of the second month (you may have to boot mom out of the house).
7. Take her on your first "show her the world" adventure – like to a hardware store – by 3 months.

By hitting these milestones you'll become an expert on taking care of your own baby. After just a few weeks of burping, swaddling, bathing, etc., taking care of him will be second nature. Your baby will also learn how dad does things. With you and him in sync, nobody in the whole world, with the possible exception of mom, will do it better.

Get to Know Your Baby

All babies are unique, and understanding your child's different characteristics will help you determine your best approach to being his dad. Characteristics include how he responds to you, a wet diaper, or hunger, and how he likes to be soothed and play. Some babies thrive on interaction, while others seem more self-contained. Some babies relax and fall asleep when you gently massage them, others become rigid and seem to be uncomfortable with a lot of touching. Noticing these responses and tuning into your child enables you to respond to his individuality and efforts to learn and explore his world.

Understanding His Emerging Personality

At 4 months your baby's temperament, the technical term for his personality or nature, is emerging sufficiently to take your understanding to the next level. Caveats from the experts include that babies continually change as they grow and what you see now is not necessarily what you'll get down the road. A beautifully behaved baby may turn into a high maintenance child, or your screamer at 3 months may be mellow at 6. Focus on his current nature, try to keep up with his changes, and stay intrigued about what the future will bring. Resources to help include:

- Babycenter.com offers their Temperament Quiz: Rate Your Baby and Yourself, which provides a great framework for understanding your baby and advice on how best to deal with you and your baby's specific characteristics.
- The Preventive Ounce (PreventiveOz. org) offers a survey tool that enables you to profile your baby beginning at 4 months and predict future behavior based on an extensive data base of the experiences of other parents.

Getting a handle on your child's temperament/personality will help guide your care strategies and interactions, as well as strengthen your sense of confidence as a capable parent.

OXYTOCIN: THE 'LOVE' HORMONE

When you first hold and stare into your baby's eyes, your brain will respond with a surge of oxytocin, the "love" homone. It drives the "amazing" feeling men report upon the birth of their child, and your brain generates more every time you hold him. You get a big booster shot by giving him a bath, and a full on blast if you lay down with him on your chest for a nap. The more you get, the more you want. His brain is tracking yours on a parallel path. That generates his smiles and excitement at three months when he sees you or just hears your voice. It is a double axle upward spiral, no doubt with a few added twists along the way, that continues for decades.

> " Having a baby entirely eliminates your life and replaces it with another one."
> — Veteran Dad

Great Ways to Bond with Your Baby

The bonding thing, whether it hits you at birth or sneaks up on you down the road, is unlike anything you've ever experienced, and it doesn't ever go away. In fact, it's what drives you to do your best as a father and makes all your sacrifices more than worthwhile. Here are some proven moves that will strengthen your bond with your new baby:

- **Use your finger as a pacifier:** Babies love to suck. A clean finger works just as well as a pacifier, and it is a surreal feeling as you actually feel instinct at work. You can also get an idea of what it is like when he latches on to mom's breast.
- **Swaddle/cuddle:** She makes a very huggable bundle when swaddled, wrapped in a blanket after a bath, or really just about any time. Hold her close to keep her warm, and give her the secure feeling that you'll always protect her.
- **Try kangaroo care:** Research found that when mothers held their premature babies to their bare chests (called kangaroo care), both of their stress levels dropped dramatically. It also works with fathers and full-term babies, and you will find that taking off your shirt and putting your soft, freshly bathed baby on your chest is pretty close to heaven.
- **Give him a bath:** Research has also found that one of the best bonding strategies for dads is giving your baby a bath. If you do it regularly, it gets very interactive, and when at several months you can take him into the bath with you,

> " A man should take every opportunity to be a part of the nighttime experience. The night-time is a magical time. Until you've sat up with your child at night while the child nurses and comes in and out of sleep, you're missing some-thing. Not to mention that your wife could use the help. You've got the rest of your life to sleep."
>
> — Veteran Dad

NEW DADS ON BONDING

"Strongest [bonding] time is when I feed him and he looks into my eyes."

"Right when they're born, and you have that time right after birth, the baby is taking everything in and getting an impression that this is mom and dad. You can be the world's worst singer, but they'll love it. The eye contact and hearing your voice – they're absorbing all that."

"For me, it was when I changed his diaper. I'd change it as often as I could because they're just look-ing at the person in front of them."

"For me, it was bath time. Just playing with toys, and generally having a really good time. She'd have a lot of fun, and then sleep really well."

it is a blast. Have mom hand him to you in the shower; socks on your hands will prevent slips and also work as wash cloths.

- **Carry her in a pouch:** Many dads report that carrying her in a soft front carrier is a great way to go. She can either snuggle in and fall asleep or look out at all of the new wonders of the world that continually pass by.
- **Take her to see your friends:** You can stay cooped up at home, or you can go visit your friends. Park your baby in the stroller near the basketball court and shoot some hoops with the guys. You will periodically interrupt your game to check on her, but your friends will be happy to help. And by taking your baby, you are scoring points all around.
- **Talk or sing to your baby:** Tell him about your day, or what he might be when he grows up. He will find everything you have to say fascinating, and when he starts babbling back, you'll be buds for life. If you sing, she will think you're the greatest. Slow tunes and lullabies are best around bedtime, but most anything you like works well for fuss prevention.
- **Get in on the feeding:** After three to four weeks of breastfeeding, encourage mom to use a breast pump so you can feed your baby with a bottle. Mom won't be tied to the baby, and it'll give her a chance to get several hours away from home and you an opportunity to really connect.

Just the Two of You

Spending time alone with your baby is the best way to build your bond and your confidence, and a great way to make the most of being a dad. So start by spending some time alone with the baby on the day he's born; encourage mom to get out alone after you bring your baby home; and when he's ready, take him out to see the world , just the two of you. Go for a long walk, take her to the park or to your favorite surfing spot. Mom will also appreciate the balance this brings to her life, and it will help strengthen your relationship with her.

AMAZING UPPER BODY STRENGTH

At one day old, a baby can almost do a pull up when he grabs onto your pinkies. At several weeks he will start lifting his head, which is half his body weight, and at a few months he can rip out a fistful of your chest hair.

DEEPLY RELAXING

You get home late, stressed out after a bad day at work. The baby is fussy and mom's had it. Life sucks, right? No, because on this night, after walking with your baby, she falls asleep on your chest, a warm little bundle sleeping like an angel. Life doesn't get any better than this.

Also see **Milestones for New Dads on page 34.**

How Can I Help My Baby Go to Sleep?

Newborns sleep for about 16 hours a day, waking up every three to four hours. Then it is time to feed and change him and give him time to explore. He will awake in the "quiet alert" phase in which he lies still and stares at things (best time for feeding). This is followed by an "active alert" phase, which is prime playtime. When he's finished playing he might let you know by looking away, arching his back or just getting cranky. He will then cry and go back to sleep and repeat the cycle.

How to Help Your Baby Go to Sleep on His Own

Trying to alter the natural schedule of a new baby to fit in with yours early on is tempting but will just lead to frustration. There are, however, constructive steps you can take to help your baby learn to go to sleep on his own. Keep in mind that every baby is different and has unique needs, both parents must buy into whatever strategy you choose, and you both must be consistent. (Same with training a puppy.)

- **Swaddle your baby** so he feels secure like he was in the womb and doesn't wake himself with his jerky leg and arm movements.
- **Make sure he has a full meal** before putting him to bed (if he drops off to sleep while feeding, dab his forehead with a wet cloth to rouse him).
- **Burp him** after his last feeding so gas pain does not wake him up. After a big burp, if mom is craving sleep, suggest she top off the tank so he might sleep longer.
- For naps during the day, keep the noise level normal and room lit, at night, be quiet with lights off (use a dim light for feeding and diaper changes), so **he will learn the difference between night and day**.
- **Put a heating pad set to low** on to the sheet when you get your baby up to nurse so the bed will be warm when you return him to it.
- **Try soft music** or recorded sound that mimics what he heard in the womb (water flowing) or try recording his own cries to play back to him.

YOU CAN'T SPOIL A NEW BABY

It's impossible for about the first year. In fact, for the first few months it is essential that you respond to your baby's cries and needs so she develops a sense of security and wellbeing.

Eventually she'll learn to cry for a variety of reasons (say, for your attention), but in the beginning every cry has a specific meaning.

> " Establish a routine, although it will probably take a couple of months. But, you should start trying to establish one and work towards sticking with it. Eventually it will work."
>
> — New Dad

- **Develop a simple bedtime routine** that in addition to feeding, diaper change and nightgown, can include a bath, massage (rub a special spot, like his forehead), or song (same one every night). Put him to sleep at the same time each night in the same place. Don't rock the baby or let mom nurse him to sleep unless this is your plan for the next year.
- At six to eight weeks, you can put him in his crib when he is groggy (e.g., rubbing eyes) but still awake to **start teaching him to drift off to sleep on his own** and "self soothe" when he wakes up at night. A little fussing before sleeping is normal.

Try a Sleep Training Technique After a Few Months

When your baby is about two to four months, you can try the sleep training method of your choice. They include the full "cry it out" method (parents let the baby cry herself to sleep without comforting her), the modified "cry it out" method (let the baby cry, but reassure her at regular intervals with a quiet pat on the back or soothing voice), and several others. Research shows they all can work, depending upon you and your baby. For the best information, look up "baby sleep training" on babycenter.com.

> " Hold your baby close, chest to chest and tap on the baby's back with two fingers, like the rythm of a heartbeat. Poom – pa-poom...he went to sleep almost every time."
>
> — Veteran Dad

Consistency is the Key

Parents should give the sleep training method of their choice seven to ten days to work before changing it. Remember that whatever you start doing ... if you keep doing it … your baby will become accustomed to it … so make sure it is something you are happy to keep doing (e.g., rocking your baby to sleep – do you want your baby to depend on this?).

Periodically invite mom to quietly check on your sleeping baby together, and marvel about your angelic little bundle. If he looks a little too quiet, go ahead and make sure he is breathing (very lightly touch his chest). We all did.

MORE SLEEP HELP

If your baby is having problems with sleeping, or you just want to learn about the tradeoffs of putting your baby on a schedule, read Healthy Sleep Habits, Happy Child by Marc Weissbluth. Great suggestions for getting your baby to sleep so you can get some too.

Troubleshooter's Guide to Crying Babies

If there is any challenge you need to take head on, it is learning to calm your crying baby. This is a job that can really put you to the test. If you get good at turning "howling like a banshee" into "sleeping like an angel," you are gold.

Fussing Peaks at Six Weeks; Getting over the Three-Month Hump

While the amount of crying varies among babies, they tend to follow similar patterns. As newborns, they generally do not cry very much. But then their crying increases steadily for several weeks and tends to plateau at 4-6 weeks. They can carry on for weeks, and then taper back down, with crying largely over by 3 months. For serious criers, it can be a very long 3 months, but then you're through the worst of it.

Troubleshooter's Guide to Crying Babies

It's the middle of the night. Your son just ate an hour ago and, for no apparent reason, has spent the last 20 minutes crying. Exhausted, mom is about to lose it. You have to go to work early but pretending to be asleep is not an option. What do you do?

No worries, we got this one down 20 years ago. The *Troubleshooter's Guide to Crying Babies* employs the same practical approach you'd use in solving car or computer problems. One of the most popular lessons at Boot Camp, it has proved effective for thousands of dads. It works because, just like when a car misfires, babies cry for a reason. Taking a proactive approach enables you to remain cool, rational and focused on finding a solution.

GET THE BASICS OF COMFORTING YOUR BABY

Most of it comes naturally, like holding, rocking, walking and singing softly. Learn from the nurses, grandma, your mate and from your own experience. Learn to distract him from what's bothering him by doing or showing him something new that re-focuses his attention.

DEVELOP A CHECKLIST OF REASONS WHY BABY CRIES

Start with the most common and add issues unique to your baby. A typical list might include:

- ❑ Hungry
- ❑ Tired
- ❑ Needs burping
- ❑ Gas/constipated
- ❑ Dirty or wet diaper
- ❑ Diaper rash
- ❑ Too hot/too cold
- ❑ Clothes rubbing
- ❑ Diaper pinching skin
- ❑ Needs to be held
- ❑ Frustrated
- ❑ Too much noise

DEVELOP A ROUTINE

Check each reason in sequence, ruling out problems as you try solutions.

CHECK FOR NEW PROBLEMS

Sometimes crying is caused by random things; his finger may be bent back in his sleeve or a hair might be wrapped around his toe. Of course, if you think your baby needs medical attention, call your doctor.

MOVE ON TO NEW TECHNIQUES

Not every problem will have a single answer. Being proactive also means trying new solutions for old problems. When you've tried everything and nothing has worked it's possible your baby is now basically "tired." After 30 minutes of crying your baby has almost certainly become overtired and simply putting him to sleep is now your main goal.

For babies with colic or if you have basic crying concerns, check out the heavy duty techniques in *Happiest Baby on the Block*.

> " There is going to be a point when you're going to run into the end of your checklist and the baby is still crying. It happens. Sometimes a baby just cries. If anything, working my way through my baby's crying has been a real test of patience for me as a father. The worst feeling is hearing your baby cry. But sometimes you also need the patience to just put the baby down and let it cry."
>
> – Veteran Dad

Ways to Calm a Crying Baby

Need more ideas? Here are some suggestions on possible fixes:

Feeding

If it's her normal feeding schedule, hand her to mom or get the bottle. If it isn't her normal time but you think she might be hungry, go for it anyway.

Changing Diaper

Make sure you treat any redness with ointment, because diaper rash hurts.

Burping

Babies can swallow air while crying, so even if she hasn't eaten in a while it's worth a shot.

Infant Swing

A battery-powered infant swing is considered essential by many. Just strap your baby in and switch it on for soothing back-and-forth motion that buys you time to get things done.

Swaddling

Crying, flailing babies can be tough, but swaddling is a proven method for calming a baby and keeping him calm.

Sucking

Put your knuckle to his lips to see if he wants to suck. If he starts going at it, pop in a pacifier or use your finger, soft side up.

Music

Music to a fussy baby is, well, music to her ears. Anything you like, in moderation, can work; if you like classical, great, but rock 'n' roll with heavy bass on low volume can work great as well. Or you can try one of the many CDs made for babies.

Bicycle Her Legs

A taut tummy or kicking legs may indicate gas or constipation, so put her on your lap facing you and gently work her legs up and down.

Hold, Walk and Rock

Walk around or rock him. Try holding him over your shoulder, face down over your arm, or face down across your lap. This puts a little pressure on his stomach, which is often soothing.

Frontpack, Backpack or Sling

Today's baby carriers provide a great opportunity for you to care for the baby while you work around the house or take a walk.

Stroller or Jogger

The vibration transmitted from the wheels traveling over the rough pavement relaxes your little one, and the fresh air helps as well. Bundle her up if it's cool outside, and make sure there is no direct sunlight hitting her face.

ONLINE RESOURCES

Colichelp.com
Good resource for helping a baby experiencing colic.
Medicinenet.com/colic/article.htm
Information on colic and possible solutions.

Bouncy Seat

Place her into the seat, propped at a 45° angle, and position it so she can see the world. It's built to gently bounce with her movements, and may have toys, music and lights to occupy your baby's developing mind.

White Noise

This can be amazingly effective for calming and lulling cranky babies to sleep. Try a hair dryer, static from a radio or record or a sleep sounds/white noise app on your phone. You can also put her baby-seat on top of a running dryer for both the vibration and white noise. Be careful not to leave, even for a moment, as the dryer's vibrations can walk her seat over the edge.

Distraction

Introduce a new toy, make a funny face, massage her ears, or blow on her forehead or neck. One veteran could always calm his crying son by taking him to see the family pets. Distraction is often the key to interrupting a cycle of crying.

Bath or Massage

Can be done routinely before bedtime to sooth and relax her. If you get her to sleep and then need to put her to bed in her crib, use a hair dryer to warm her bedding a little so the shock of cold sheets doesn't wake her up.

Ride in the Car

A classic technique used by dads when their babies are crying. The vibration and noise will put most babies to sleep within the first mile or so.

Fussy Baby

Call the Fussy Baby Network warmline at 1-888-431-BABY(2229) and get questions answered or go to fussybabynetwork.org for more information.

WHEN TO PUT HIM DOWN AND WALK AWAY

Sometimes he is just on another crying jag and there isn't anything you can do to calm him. If that's the case, leave him be for a while. It might seem harsh, but his crying is one way for him to get his system back in sync. Vigorous crying is physically exhausting for a baby, and several minutes of it can actually help him sleep once he does go down.

They may be fleeting, but episodes of extreme frustration due to a crying baby are exceptionally dangerous. If you feel yourself losing control, put the baby down in the safety of his crib and walk away. Never react in anger. It is incredibly easy to permanently damage an infant's brain and shaking a baby can even lead to death. Just walk away before incessant crying pushes you to that point.

How Your Baby Grows and Develops

Incredible Brain Development

While the typical infant spends two-thirds of her day sleeping and the rest eating, crying, pooping and staring into space, there is also an amazing process underway inside her brain. At birth a baby's brain contains 100 billion neurons (all the nerve cells she will ever have) but the cells are not "programmed." Sensory experiences involving sight, smell, touch, etc., are what connect the neurons and "program" the brain for functions like language, vision, understanding, and coordination.

Just after birth, her brain produces trillions of connections between neurons and begins stimulating those that will be used and eliminating those that won't. Every stimulant helps forge a path between her brain cells, much like an electrical grid that connects neighborhoods and cities. Rich experiences produce rich brains. Like a muscle, a baby's brain increases its capability based on how much it's used.

Help Your Baby Grow

A stimulating environment doesn't mean flash cards, videos, or the many other commercial products being pushed on new parents who want to give their child the best possible start in life. What it does mean is deceptively simple: babies learn by reacting to the sights, sounds, smells and shapes around them. They also learn by meeting challenges put before them – reaching, grabbing, and getting you to pay attention. As a father, you can bring a different set of learning experiences than mom to your baby's world. Stimulate your baby by talking to her, touching her, being affectionate, showing her the world around her, and introducing objects for her to see, feel, taste, and experience.

THE MYTH OF MOZART

A study in the 1990s played Mozart for 10 minutes to students about to take an IQ test. The students IQ's improved an average of 8 points and their spatial, temporal reasoning improved temporarily. The media got a hold of this and it wasn't long until moms-to-be were playing Mozart to their babies in the womb. The study authors pointed out the results showed the benefits of relaxation, not that Mozart made developing brains smarter, but the notion persists today in products marketed to new parents.

> When I come home she is doing something new or different everyday. She crawls a little better, she pulls up on things. Starting about 3-4 months, you will really start to notice that."
>
> – Veteran Dad

Play with Your Baby

Start early, as having fun is the best brain developer of all. This includes letting her grasp your finger, showing your baby her reflection in a mirror, and making new sounds for her to figure out. Play improves her senses and muscle development and control, and builds her sense of inner excitement. Never underestimate the power of play. For example, the skills a three-month old baby learns by playing a simple game of "peek-a-boo!" include observation, language, coordination, communication, exploration, problem solving, socialization, creativity and humor. Other games work on physical factors like dexterity, balance, trust, strength and timing. Repetition will enhance your baby's learning of new games and skills.

Talk, Sing and Read

Your voice can soothe and delight. Babies pick up inflections, gestures, and start to understand storytelling at a young age. Some will utter nonsensical sounds mimicking you. Talk to her about daily events, sports, news, your job; anything at all. Sing and read as well. Use a variety of high and low pitches, loud and soft tones.

Nurture an Adventurous Spirit

Notice when he's reaching out for something and encourage his exploration. Let him take his time. Let him try for something just beyond his reach. Before you do something for him, let him try to do it himself. Encourage but don't frustrate, or you run the risk of diminishing his natural inquisitiveness and motivation. And never scare a baby; the effects will inhibit rather than nurture his adventurous spirit.

Improvise

Put your own creative stamp on playing with your baby; build your repertoire of games that only she and you know. Opportunities abound: Make your sock into a puppet and make it "sing" to him. Start to blow raspberries a couple of times on his tummy and then stop until he is bouncing with anticipation. Then cut loose with a big one. Let her splash in the bath – on you. Lay down on your back, sit him on your chest, and let him explore your face, check out how your beard feels, and grab your nose. Go roller blading while pushing him in the stroller (slowly). Let her strum your guitar.

> " If you like Mozart and play it for your baby in the womb, he won't get any smarter than if you rap or introduce him to rock and roll. But all three, or anything else you like, will make him smarter, as the more stimulus for his growing brain, the better. He will also recognize your favorite music upon arrival and is apt to like it too. Bottom line is, anything you do with your baby is a good thing."
>
> — Veteran Dad

Show Your Baby The World

Why He Picks You for Play

It starts right after birth when your bright little bundle notices that you look, smell, feel and sound different than mom. Your baby won't know what to think of you right off, which is why he stares at you so much. As the weeks go by, a baby notices that mom tends to be protective and calming, while dad is more playful, physical, and often surprising. Your baby soon learns that mom will pick him up when he is fussy, but dad will tickle him or lift him in the air. When even a very young baby hears his father's voice he's likely to raise his shoulders and eyebrows, or begin kicking his legs, in anticipation of some excitement. Playing teaches him how to laugh and take risks. It develops his motor skills and speeds the development of his brain and nervous system. Very serious stuff, and just what dads are for.

Mom and Dad: Complementary Roles for Raising Babies

While they can come into conflict, a father's adventurous role complements that of a mother's, and the combination is what turns out well-rounded children. Dads introduce new challenges to their babies and encourage them to explore their worlds. Bottom line, playtime with dad contributes to your baby's physical, intellectual, and social development, and leads to great qualities later in life: good relationships with peers, a knowledge of limits, a spirit of adventure.

> " For in the child lies the future of the world. Mother must hold him close so he knows it is his world. Father must take the child to the highest hill so he can see what his world is like."
>
> – Mayan Proverb

Show Him the World

As chief adventure officer in your new family, this is your job. Babies are incredibly curious and will become still, watchful, and even mesmerized with anything new to check out. If he is fussy, this is a great way to distract.

Start by carrying him against your chest facing out, with one hand under his bottom and the other over his chest, with his head resting against you. Or get a front carrier and face him out. Just walk around slowly, positioning him so new things come into his field of vision. It doesn't matter what it is; just watch his face to see what captures his attention. Describe it to him in a soft voice and just let him take it in.

Around the house: Start with wallpaper and a light switch and move on to pictures, mirrors (always interesting) and windows. The kitchen is full of interesting stuff, so take your time and open the cupboards one at a time. A garden with flowers is great; let her check them out and touch them (careful she doesn't try to eat them). Bugs are very cool as they crawl around; ditto on the eating.

Away from home: Every new place presents new opportunities; someone else's house, the neighborhood, a park, mall, or even a truck dealer. Getting fussy at a restaurant? Show him the pictures in the hall, or take a walk outside where you can introduce him to cool cars. Make sure the diaper bag is fully stocked for an outing that will last more than a few hours, and when it is nap time, wrap him up in a familiar blanket from his crib and hold him so he gets warm and falls asleep.

Hardware store baby tour: It's hard to imagine a place with more interesting stuff for a baby to check out than a hardware store; aisle after aisle with lots of colors, tools and materials you can tell her about. Be careful she doesn't get close enough to grab things, but letting her get the feel of a hammer while you firmly hold the hammer's head in your hand is fine.

BABIES ARE EASILY ENTERTAINED

"What I hadn't realized is that it doesn't have to be anything big to entertain him. Just walking around the backyard and pointing things out keeps his attention."

— New Dad

" When women dream about having a baby, they dream about this cute, chubby little infant. When guys dream about having a kid, they always dream about adolescents, and things they're going to do with them, like taking them fishing, or playing sports, or things like that. It's really true ... I never had any visions of me, like, holding a two month old."

— Veteran Dad

First Year Escapades for Dads & Babies

1st Quarter

BABY...	DAD...	DEVELOPS...
Follows things with eyes	Slowly moves bright objects side-to-side close to his face, and then up and down.	Visual skills, peripheral vision
Responds to sounds	Talk to her with different tones of voice and sing to her (she'll "coo" back sooner).	Sound differentiation, recognition
Intrigued by textures	Let her feel and explore your face, and things with textures around the house.	Tactile senses, exploration
Sees at close range	Show him his face in a mirror, make faces, stick out tongue. Baby may imitate you.	Perception, facial expression
Lifts head when on belly	Get nose-to-nose and talk to him; make tummy time fun, encourage mini-pushups.	Upper body and core strength
Tightly grasps things	Lie her on your lap and let her grasp your little fingers to do pull-ups as you talk.	Arm strength and coordination
Smiles, coos, laughs	Smile and laugh back. When he coos at you, mimic him (he'll "light up).	Verbal skills, sense of humor
Sees color and distance	Turn out the lights, turn on a flashlight and shine it on colorful things in room.	Observation, inquisitiveness

2nd Quarter

BABY...	DAD...	DEVELOPS...
Can stand while held	Stand her on your lap as she squats and jumps through full range of motion.	Leg strength, fast twitch muscles
Reaches for, grabs objects	Tour house with him in a front carrier and let him grab and feel safe things within his reach.	Hand-to-eye coordination
Rolls over	Put her on a blanket on the floor and place a toy just out of reach.	Strength, flexibility, determination
Imitates sounds	Sing a lullaby, rock 'n' roll or drinking song; repetition and enthusiasm are key.	Language skills, concentration
Moves objects hand to hand	Start him on blocks; let him bang them, build him something to knock down, help him build.	Fine muscle-control, creativity
Puts toes in her mouth	Dip her big toe in your ice cream cone and pop it in her mouth a few times.	Flexibility, surprise, delight
Inspects objects in detail	Give her interesting things/pictures of faces to inspect; point out features/names.	Ability to focus, attention span

3rd Quarter

BABY...	DAD...	DEVELOPS...
Sits up without support	Invest in a backpack baby carrier and go on hiking adventures; start short.	Fascination with outdoors
Feeds himself	Let him use his hands and then guide his hand holding a spoon; prepare for a mess.	Independence, coordination
Crawls, scoots or rolls	Crawlers have 4-wheel drive, build an offroad course with cushions and sheets.	Strength, agility, motivation
Upper body strength	Roll her over and back, let her grab your face, raspberries on her tummy.	Strength, trust, toughness
Jabbers away	Jabber back with delight; read her anything; tell jokes; notice her jabber cadence.	Communication, personality
Learns objects' names	Tell names of things; ball, nose, toes, "da da", etc.; repeat regularly; cheer her on.	Language formation
Walks holding onto things	Set up a track where she can fall safely; encourage exploration by putting her toys out.	Exploration, determination
Bangs and throws things	Skills dads excel at! Start a kitchen band, play retriever to his throws, roll ball back.	Enthusiasm for sports, music

4th Quarter

BABY...	DAD...	DEVELOPS...
Finds hidden objects	Start with peek-a-boo, then teach her to find toys and other treasures.	Problem solving, motivation
Imitates you	Teach him "high five," touchdown, etc.; develop a "secret handshake".	Learning skills, socialization
Starts to say words	Your reaction to "da da" will quickly teach her to work you for all you are worth.	Communication, people skills
Stands, starts walking	She will be amazed at first; keep her safe, eventually play "I'm gonna get you."	Balance, risk taking, anticipation
Puts toys away (really)	Teach him to play "cleanup": Babies like to pull things out,put them in containers.	Following directions, patience
"Draws" with a crayon	Encourage your budding artist; let her chose a color and you can color along.	Imagination, fine motor skills
Loves balls, bathtime and flying	Go for it; balls everywhere, toys in the tub, and airplane rides complete with sound effects.	Desire to have great fun with dad

Starting a Life Long Love Affair

After a century or so of baby care being considered "women's work," men collectively don't have a lot of experience with infants. So it will be a pleasant surprise when the notion that men are inherently ignorant and incapable with babies evaporates the first time you rock yours to sleep in your arms. There will be many other pleasant surprises too, like the first time she smiles at you, says "da da," and gets excited to see you. You start getting the impression that not only does this little thing like you, when it comes to the "big guy" in her life, only you will do. Even if her cries irritate you, once she falls asleep on your shoulder, snuggling into you for warmth and protection, you feel very lucky to have her.

First Wonder of Your World

Considering the billions of babies born over the millennia, it seems impossible that any one of them could be special. But yours will be. Your baby represents your own immortality, and the future of mankind, and the meaning of your life – not to mention her own unique and incredible potential as a human being. Accepting the enormity presented by your child can take you years.

Babies can also Be Boring, Frustrating and Irritating

Babies can be a wonderful source of happiness, but there's a flip side. It just goes with the territory, especially if you're unsure of how to care for and play with them. In any situation, there's always something that you haven't tried that may work, and the more you try, the better you will get. Your ability to maintain a positive attitude will be tied to your competence, and that comes from knowing that there is always something more that can be tried to quiet your crying baby or put your tired baby to sleep.

> "You get into an upward spiral – he gets to know you, you feel great – play more, he smiles more, etc. You have bad days but it always keeps getting better."
> — Veteran Dad

Courting Your Baby

The notion of courtship between a father and his baby is a good analogy, because it's a relationship that needs to develop, and this will take time. Seek out the opportunities early on to take her out with you, tell her about your world, and defend her from all threats. These actions create true love, and if the opportunities are consistently pursued, a very deep and enduring relationship is the result. The more time you spend with your baby, the better you will know her and the more she will respond to you.

Start a Lifelong Love Affair

The regular expression of love and encouragement to your child is the most important practice you can develop. We tend to be more critical of ourselves than others, and we extend this to our children, especially our firstborn. While at times negative feedback may be appropriate with her, the rule should be regular expressions that are very positive. Your child's self esteem, motivation, and zest for life to a large extent will correlate with how positive you are in her upbringing. Saying "I love you" often will also become a self fulfilling prophecy on both ends.

This practice ultimately becomes a habit, and is one that should start on day one of your child's life. With your child in your arms, look into his eyes and gently murmur how beautiful he is. When he grabs your finger, tell him how strong he is. If he burps, tell him what a good burper he is. Crying indicates healthy lungs, and potential as a singer.

> " A lot of people will say, 'Well, what is it you guys do with the baby?' I have staring contests. He's my psychiatrist. I come home with my work problems and he listens. I mean, you do all kinds of things with them. They're just really fun."
>
> — Veteran Dad

Crying at night indicates a partier. You get the idea – your child can do no wrong.

Nothing Like Knowing You Were There When It Counted

Tough babies, like those with colic, present a special opportunity for dads. We have no choice but to get involved with their care, but it is over at around three months and then you have decades knowing that you were there for her when she needed you. Not a bad way to start your legacy as a father.

CHAPTER 4

Caring For New Moms

" It's important to remember that women are under a lot of pressure to be perfect moms. They think they should have that innate ability to mother their baby."
— Veteran Dad

Basic Biology of New Moms

Our 20 year quest to understand new moms was energized by Louann Brizendine, MD, a leading neuroscientist and mom who confirmed that "motherhood…literally changes a woman's brain - structurally, functionally, and in many ways, irreversibly." While your mate's beliefs and characteristics will also shape her as a mom, the innate biological changes she experiences will surprise her and impact the choices she makes and the direction she takes. A magical mystery tour for both of you.

She explained as a leading neuroscientist that a mom's biology developed as a means of the survival for our species, and as a mom herself, how it works:

- "Deeply buried in my genetic code were triggers for basic mothering behavior that were primed by the hormones of pregnancy, activated by childbirth and reinforced by close physical contact with my child."
- "These physical cues from her infant forge new neuro-chemical pathways in her brain that create and reinforce maternal brain circuits aided by chemical imprinting and huge increases of oxytocin."
- "These changes result in a motivated, highly attentive and aggressively protective brain that forces the new mother to alter

> " There's you before kids and there's you after kids and they're not the same person."
>
> — Jennifer Lopez, performer, mother of two

her responses and priorities in life. She is relating to this person in a way she has never related to anyone else in her life. The stakes are life and death."

- "Biology can hijack our brain circuits despite our best intentions. Even the most career oriented woman's, changing the way she thinks, feels and what she finds important."

We have always heard the veterans talk about how they brought two new people home from the hospital, and now we know why. In the midst of the jumble of issues and events of bringing a new baby into this world, your mate will give her complete commitment to your child, so be aware as it is beautiful to see.

> " Even if he does the bathing, etc, I'm still watching. I never really relax."
>
> — New Mom

She Has Cave Mom's Instinct and Biological Imperative

A mom's basic biology is shared by most mammals and developed over eons; for humans it culminated in the cave mom, who with cave dads formed "mating pairs" and worked together every day to keep their kids alive and flourishing. Not much different than today in some respects, but our tribe has spread out.

The upside is clear; but with saber-tooths gone, grocery stores around and central heating in our caves, today's moms still can't lighten up and back off. It is literally not in their DNA.

Sarah Schoppe-Sullivan, PhD, a professor (and mom) specializing in how new parents work together in their new family, has added a critical perspective on the impacts of mom's biology on new fathers:

"Mothers are in the driver's seat … and can encourage fathers and open the gate to their involvement in child care, or be very critical and close the gate." She explained that moms-to-be who want to share the baby with dad often change their minds when junior and her hormone surges show up , and if dad wants to be highly involved, he will back off in the face of serious criticism from mom. These feelings persist and moms and dads who split child care have more conflicts than when mom is the primary caregiver.

Sarah's takeaway? New parents need to learn together from the experience of other new families, and since no one size fits all, decide for themselves what works best for their family.

> " My husband finally stopped doing things. He said I was just going to do them over."
>
> — New Mom

How To Support A Mom-To-Be

By far the most prevalent advice from our veteran dads is to "take care of mom; no matter what she is experiencing, no matter how tough she is on you, take care of her." Start early in her pregnancy, here is how you do it:

Talk to Her

About the baby, her thoughts and concerns, yours too, your plans as a family, and make it a habit to ask how she is doing. Even if she seems to be handling pregnancy okay, don't underestimate its impact upon her. Just the two of you talking is the best way to prepare to be a family, and if you are a man of few words, make a list of topics so you don't run out of things to say.

Walk with Her

Pregnancy will limit her physical activity and your nightlife, but instead of just sitting around together watching TV, invite her to take walks with you. It benefits her moods, makes the birth easier and gives her a head start on getting her body back afterward. You could probably use some exercise as well, and walking and talking go hand-in-hand.

Show Her that You Care

Men tend to be creative, and this is a great time for thinking outside the box to show her that you care about her and the baby. If she develops a craving for ice cream, call her from the ice cream store and read her the flavors. Make a cradle for your baby if you can, or paint stars and rainbows on the ceiling in the nursery. Use your imagination.

Get up to Speed on Her Symptoms

You will never keep up with her reading, but if you at least scan one of her favorite books, you will surprise and please her with your knowledge. And you can use it to help her cope.

DON'T TAKE IT PERSONALLY

Mom's hormone-driven mood swings and frustration are the norm. It's no fun, but serving as her punching bag to help exorcise her frustrations is just one of our jobs. Remind her (and yourself) of their natural cause and that they will pass. Help her get rest, time alone, and exercise. Reassure her it will all work out and she will be a great mom, count to 10, and don't get sucked into arguments.

> On the internet – be careful. People like to complain. My wife would go on these forums and she'd get worried about every little thing. People don't go to make posts to tell you how awesome everything is. They go to tell you how terrible everything went."
>
> — Veteran Dad

Go to Her Doctor Visits

This is the single most important thing you can do during pregnancy, as visits with her obstetrician get you personally connected with what's going on both with mom and baby. Being there lets mom know she isn't alone. If you are unable to go to any visit be sure to ask her what happened. When you are with the doctor, don't be shy about asking questions. If you're being ignored, be assertive, but keep the focus on mom. Make sure she is getting all of her questions asked and answered.

Help Her Through the Pregnancy

The physical and emotional impacts of her pregnancy may be intense, and if so she will depend on you to help her get through the roughest times. It may be up to you to save her from herself as she's started on the second jar of pickles, or if she's sneaking a cigarette in the bathroom. A few ideas on how you can help; ask her for others:

- **Morning Sickness:** It hits most new moms, comes early in her pregnancy and can happen any time of day. While food may seem to be the problem, eating food that she can handle is the antidote.

Brainstorm with her on foods she might try (nuts, fruits, vegetables) and indulge her cravings by keeping them stocked. Encourage her to eat smaller meals more frequently, to eat slowly, and stay hydrated. If she looks like she may lose her lunch, help her get to the bathroom and help her clean up.

- **Backache:** Weight gain, a shifting center of gravity, inactivity, inability to stretch, and a growing baby pushing her pelvic structure open all conspire to produce back problems. Due to their effect on the baby, painkillers are generally not permitted. You can help by giving her back rubs. Use the best technique you can muster by asking her how and where to rub. Help her find support straps for pregnant moms that lift her belly and a body pillow so she can swing one leg and arm over it while sleeping.

- **Sore Breasts:** They start growing early in pregnancy and keep growing, often causing pain and tenderness. If so, suggest a special pregnancy support bra. Offer to massage them, perhaps using her stretch mark prevention lotion; stay away from her nipples. Pour her a warm bath. Be very gentle in love making; if she asks, place her breasts "off limits" until the soreness subsides.

> **❝❝** Do anything you can to help your wife go through the process of being a mother. Even though it's more natural for her, it also requires an adjustment that's much greater for a woman because there are demands being put on her body that you don't experience. So the best thing to do is swallow your own point of view for awhile and just be there."
>
> — Veteran Dad

Her Transformation into a Mom

Millenniums of evolution and socialization have a powerful impact upon our mates when they conceive our baby. They are hard wired and biologically driven to develop an intense bond, which causes them to sacrifice a great deal as they carry, give birth and care for our child. Many of us wish we had a similar bond right away, but knowing she is giving our child a tremendous gift should outweigh any envy we feel. Our bond will come in time.

Over the initial year, motherhood will change her to her core. If you track her changes month-by-month as described in pregnancy books, you'll easily lose the forest in the trees. For what happens to her goes way beyond morning sickness and breastfeeding; she is virtually reborn as a mother who unconditionally commits herself to the well-being of our child.

This metamorphosis of a woman into a mother is one of the most remarkable of all human experiences. It warrants our deep respect, but it's easy to take for granted. The more you understand, the better you can help bring out the best in her as a mom, and as a partner. You will find that in time she does the same for you as a dad.

Our Unique Perspective: A Few Things We've Learned

Over the years, we have witnessed many thousands of new moms, and a few things we have learned include:

- Motherhood is indeed beautiful, particularly as your wife absorbs the reality of a baby growing inside her and holds him after he is born. But it can also wreak havoc on her mind, soul and body. It also may not, so don't assume anything and tune into what is actually happening to her.

- She can experience a long, tough and tumultuous ride, a physical and emotional gauntlet of thrills, pain, fierce love, depression, exhaustion, frustration and fulfillment. Since you are along for the ride, go with the flow, share in it and help her when you can; know that you cannot fix everything.
- As with fathers, a child pushes mothers to mature into better people, just in a much shorter time frame.
- The woman you love is still there, and if you play your cards right, in time you will get much of her back. Plus a lot more in the form of a mom for your baby.

First Babies Can Be Tough on Moms

Some new mothers would have it no other way; being a mom just fits. But for most, it is a roller coaster ride of ups and downs. Many women's modern, fast-paced lives aren't geared toward caring for a baby who will cry, nurse, and poop at all hours. Add a mother's innate, intense focus on her baby, and you will likely have some real stress and even misery. And don't forget the hormones, which supercharge her feelings, causing exhaustion and disorientation.

New Moms Can Be Tough on New Dads

New dads are generally way behind moms on the pregnancy learning curve, and she might be concerned that you won't be there when it counts. Her body, emotions, identity, sense of worth; her very being gets wrapped around her baby. How much energy and attention will your sweetheart have left over for you? Who is the readily available target for her mood swings and frustrations? And she may feel like she is the only one having a hard time, "he's not going to be there for me, he wants me to make all the career sacrifices, all he wants to do is have sex…" It just goes with the territory.

Window of Opportunity for Fathers

Birth is when it gets real. Not only is this when she needs you most, but once the baby arrives your support is what she'll remember in the years ahead. Bottom line – your performance during this crucial post-birth period will form the basis for her new perspective of you as the father of her child and her partner as a parent. Given the stakes, no investment of your support and perseverance during the first several months can be too much, so dig deep.

"One of the biggest things was she was hypersensitive. They get it ingrained in their minds that they're supposed to know everything about taking care of a child, but in reality, they can be just as clueless as we are, but they can't share that because they expect themselves to know everything"

– Veteran Dad

Her Pregnancy by Trimester

This overview gives you the rundown on what to expect during her pregnancy by every 3-month-period (trimester), so consider this the "Cliffs notes" to her 500-page, month-by-month version (which gives her even more to worry about by covering every possible problem she or her baby can experience). Stay tuned in to what she is experiencing and look for opportunities to help her through pregnancy.

First Trimester

From the point of conception, her body begins to react even though her pregnancy is not apparent. A wide range of symptoms can accompany pregnancy; some of the physical and emotional changes that she is likely to experience in the first three months are:

❑ Nausea and vomiting
❑ Frequent urination
❑ Tiredness
❑ Breast tenderness
❑ Mood swings
❑ Odd tastes, cravings
❑ Heightened sense of smell
❑ Weight gain

During the first trimester it is imperative for mom to take care of herself. No smoking or alcohol, good nutrition, prenatal vitamins, moderate exercise, and plenty of rest make for a healthy pregnancy. If she does not have one, she needs to find a doctor (ask around). She should make an appointment for her first prenatal visit at about eight weeks. If at any time you have concerns about your mate's condition — unusual pain, bleeding, etc. — *call her doctor.*

Prenatal care is essential as this is the most crucial time in your baby's development. This is also when he is most vulnerable to harm from alcohol, x-rays and other toxins, so help her stay informed and protected.

Second Trimester

In the next three months, some of her first trimester symptoms like nausea and fatigue tend to subside, although not entirely. They are replaced by a variety of new symptoms:

❑ Renewed energy
❑ Emotional contentment
❑ First fetal movements
❑ Headaches
❑ Heartburn
❑ Hemorrhoids
❑ Constipation
❑ Leg cramps, especially at night
❑ Swelling of legs, feet, and hands
❑ Skin, hair, and nails change
❑ Clumsiness, forgetfulness
❑ Impaired vision
❑ Faintness, dizziness
❑ Varicose veins

Her body is definitely taking on a pregnant shape, and she'll probably need to start wearing loose or maternity clothes. She should have her energy back, and with it a sense of emotional well being. She may feel a return of libido (enjoy it while you can!). She'll be feeling the baby move now. Wait a few more weeks, and you will too.

> " I have also learned to have patience with my wife; she's got a lot of hormones running through her and has a lot of apprehensions too. I'm the one with the easy job of being able to kind of sit back, and she is the one who is actually pregnant."
>
> — Rookie Dad

Third Trimester

In the final three months, her previous symptoms continue and magnify:

- ☐ Frequent and urgent urination
- ☐ Hip and pelvic pains
- ☐ Backaches
- ☐ Sleeplessness
- ☐ Shortness of breath
- ☐ Impatience and frustration
- ☐ Braxton-Hicks (false) contractions
- ☐ Anxiety over delivery
- ☐ Disturbing dreams about baby

Although she's in the home stretch, she feels more anxious now than ever, with her energy level dropping and concerns about preparedness rising. She may waiver between feeling completely enthusiastic and completely anxious. Birth preparation classes are standard and important, not only so you'll both understand what to expect during labor and delivery, but also to ease your fears of the unknown.

As D-Day Approaches

The last few weeks are when she needs you the most, since many moms get scared of giving birth. Plan on spending most of your time with her, avoid trips away if possible, and stay in touch by phone. If she is working during this period (doctors routinely place moms on disability near the due date), she may have no desire to go and may find it difficult to focus.

NEW DADS ON...
... LABOR AND DELIVERY

"Cutting the cord doesn't hurt the baby or mother, but it's tough, like calamari."

"If you love your wife, it's going to be really hard to see her in pain during labor. There's not too much that can really prepare you for this."

... NEW MOMS

"You should work together with your wife to set some boundaries up for after the baby comes, like who visits, how involved the grandmas are going to be, etc."

"Some new mothers cry about anything and you have to be patient because it doesn't make sense. As men we feel like we need to fix it."

"This last month has probably been the toughest because she's become more hormonal. But, I just do the best that I can and don't engage in the little fights. They'll be started, but just let them roll off your back."

— Veteran Dad

Caring for a New Mom

Most new mothers struggle in the first few weeks or months. She needs to physically recover from pregnancy and childbirth, her emotions still can run rampant, she gets no more than a few hours rest at a time, and she may feel trapped or virtually chained to the baby. It can be worse, so review *Baby Blues & Postpartum Depression on page 64* and be prepared for whatever happens.

Her Expectations of Herself May Exceed Reality

A new mom will get more than tired; she can suffer from extreme fatigue. It's caused not only by the unpredictability of the baby waking to nurse every few hours, but also by the constant pressure of feeling she is responsible for her baby's survival. Exhausted and overwhelmed, she may feel she is expected to inherently know what to do with a crying infant and be as happy as a little girl playing with her favorite doll. Make sure you don't expect this, and that she knows it.

> " It's about being there at the right time and doing the right thing. When you come home give mom a kiss first, then the baby. Start the baby's bath and give mom time to reenergize."
>
> – Veteran Dad

Her Maternal Instincts Will Kick In

In time her maternal instincts will kick in. It will boost her confidence, which in turn will allow her to relax. As she learns to trust her instincts and steadily develops confidence, the realization that she is a real mom will set in. She will take on the aura of one who has been tested and has proven herself, and will become a mother in her own mind. It is an awesome transformation. Your encouragement and reassurance will help her get there.

How to Support a New Mom

All new mothers are different, and the one in your life may react in ways that surprise you. Be prepared early on to support her in a big way. No advice from veteran fathers is more commonly heard or strongly held than "take care of mom; no matter what, give her all the support you can."

Basic suggestions from veteran dads for helping mom in the first few weeks include:
- Quickly learn to change diapers, burp, and calm your crying baby. Show mom she can count on you.
- Coordinate help. Obtain what you need from family, friends or neighbors, and make sure it is actually helpful.
- Help her get some sleep when the baby is sleeping and when you take him for a walk in the stroller.
- Let her know that you don't expect her to be a fairy tale mom.
- In the middle of the night when the baby is crying and both of you are dead tired, find the strength to get up and handle the baby so mom can sleep.
- Impromptu backrubs leave her feeling loved and appreciated.
- An encouraging afternoon call home when your baby is fussy and mom is frustrated can mean a lot.
- Take a little time each day to talk about something other than the baby, especially how mom is feeling.

She expects herself to be a great mom, because anything less would mean she is depriving her baby of something he needs. Your job is to help her do her best, and to make sure she feels good about her ability to give her baby all he needs. It can take some time before this realization sets in with her.

> " My wife had a c-section and was breastfeeding, so I decided to take on the role of making sure the house looked good. My wife is sort of type A and if the house gets untidy, she starts to think of all that she needs to do. So I decided to take that on. But after a couple of weeks or so, she looked at me and said "Why won't you do anything with the baby?" I thought I was doing exactly what she needed, but it turned out she needed a combination of the two. So, keep communicating."
>
> – Veteran Dad

Help Her Succeed as a Mom

Help Her Bond with Her Baby

Don't be surprised or disappointed if your mate does not mimic the stereotypical mother who falls in love with her baby at first sight. While moms tend to bond faster than dads, many experience difficulties developing a deep emotional attachment with their babies. In fact, women sometimes experience weeks of tortured insecurity and doubt about their ability to love this needy, crying, demanding and incomprehensible child.

Sometimes it only takes a sympathetic ear or even a good laugh to dispel the myths of automatic bonding and unqualified love. Let her know that her feelings are more normal than society's unrealistic expectations of her to be some kind of saint. To help her connect and develop confidence in her capabilities as a mother, point out all the things she does right for the baby. Encourage her to touch, cuddle and engage in regular skin-to skin contact with the baby.

Mothers who get a late start on bonding move on to develop as strong a relationship with their babies as those who get an early start. Moving forward is the objective, and getting overly anxious over bonding can become an obstacle along her path; so help her lighten up on herself and do the little things that help make it happen, like giving her a break.

Reassure and Encourage Her

A mom can feel incompetent or even guilty when she cannot calm her crying baby because her "maternal instinct" is supposed to tell her exactly why the baby is crying and how to comfort him. Being dead tired, feeling fat and unattractive, having little control over her own emotions, and seeing no end in sight can make her plight seem hopeless.

PROVING YOU'LL BE THERE

"Start showing that you want to be there, you want to feed the kid, you want to change the diaper, you want to take the kid. Just me coming [to Boot Camp for New Dads] today and going 'You know what? Take the morning off – I want to spend some time with my daughter.' She was like 'I can go to the gym right now? Sweet!' She was extremely excited about that. Just showing that you want to be there – that's 90% of what they're worried about. Because they know that they can take care of the baby. But it's what you can do."

— Veteran Dad

" Us dads aren't supposed to know anything. And moms, well moms are supposed to automatically know everything."

— Veteran Dad

Encouragement and support by dad is essential. Point out what a great job she is doing, what a wonderful baby she produced, and how much you appreciate her. The more support, the better the mom. Assure her that you are in it together and you will get through it together. Be positive, constructive, and help build her confidence. Keep in mind she is in a process, and that you can't nag her into motherhood. Build her up instead.

Help Her Deal with Isolation

After a month or so, the excitement over the baby's birth winds down, the calls and visits taper off, and mom no longer attracts much attention.

❑ Encourage contact with other mothers (friends, neighbors, her mom, in-laws, birth classmates) who can provide guidance and a strong sense of security. Others in a similar situation will serve as a readily available support system.

❑ Encourage her to join a new moms group where she will connect with other moms who fully understand her situation, are highly sympathetic, and have lots of ideas and advice she can trust.

❑ Encourage her to get out. Although babies tend to be portable, going out with a newborn can be so much work that it may not happen as often as it should.

Recognize Her "Gatekeeping" for What it Is

A mother has an intense relationship with her baby, and it's not always easy, even if she is exhausted, for her to share him with you. There you are, primed and ready to do your part, and she's hovering over you, scrutinizing everything you try to do. What do you do if your wife wants to do everything herself?

❑ Remind her that you need the practice. Let her know how important being close to your son or daughter is to you, right from the beginning. Stand your ground gently, and suggest she'll be glad for your involvement in the long run.

❑ If she's constantly looking over your shoulder and correcting you, take the baby into another room. Get out alone with your baby to prove to her that you are fully capable of taking care of your own child.

❑ Understand that her life is wrapped around the baby, and her "control freak" behavior is tied directly to her desire to do a good job as a mother.

Things will balance out in time if you keep pressing to be involved.

> " Recognize that you'll have those moments when you just need to walk away. With my wife and I, I feel like I'm a little bit more levelheaded and I can see her getting overwhelmed at times, so it's good to have that conversation up front and let her know she's got an open door. If she ever feels overwhelmed, there's no problem with her coming and saying, 'Hey, I need to get away.' Because I don't want her to feel like she's giving up, or she's failed."
>
> — Veteran Dad

Baby Blues & Postpartum Depression

The Baby Blues

The baby blues generally occur between birth and 6 weeks, and about 80% of new moms experience them in some way. A drop in hormone levels following delivery can be aggravated by being overly tired, going back to work, feeling inadequate as a mom, feeling trapped/isolated and problems bonding with the baby. Symptoms include mood swings, anxiety, irritability, insomnia, crying, nervousness, and general unhappiness. Once mom and baby settle into a routine (after several weeks), and her hormone levels stabilize, the baby blues usually disappear.

What You Can Do

Your job is to remain supportive and find ways to lighten her load. Encourage her to talk about what is going on and remind her it's normal and will pass. Insist she get out of the house and away from the baby. If the problems persist some professional help may be in order, so talk to your physician. It's paramount to take care of emotional problems quickly because once they become more entrenched these problems will be even more difficult to deal with.

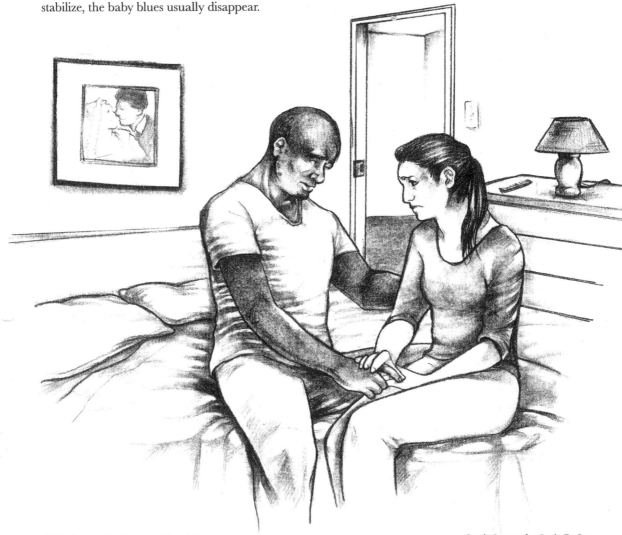

Postpartum Depression

Up to 20% of new mothers develop full blown postpartum depression, which typically occurs between six weeks and one year after childbirth. This is a medical problem, and women with a family or personal history of depression are more likely to suffer from it. If some of the following symptoms persist for more than a week notify your spouse's obstetrician or a helpline at the hospital immediately and discuss your concerns:

- Insomnia or sleeping too much
- Loss of appetite or overeating
- A lack of interest in activities
- Inability to concentrate
- Extreme mood swings
- Lethargy or hyperactivity
- Feelings of helplessness
- Panic attacks
- Disorientation and confusion
- Hopelessness or lack of control
- Inability to care for herself or baby
- Loss of touch with reality

What You Can Do

As a new father it is extremely important to know the signs of depression. You will have to take action on your mate's behalf if you suspect that she is slipping beyond the baby blues into true postpartum depression. Because of mom's isolation at home, you may be the only one to even notice these symptoms. She is ill and requires medical attention; essential steps to take are:

- Take care of your baby and consider asking for help from friends and relatives.
- Immediately consult professional help for your wife by an experienced counselor or her physician.
- Get educated on postpartum depression with information from her doctor, hospital or online.
- Talk to her about postpartum depression, about how she feels, as well as about how you feel.
- Get involved in her treatment by going with her to visit the doctor and/or therapist.
- Call in the reinforcements: reach out to family, friends and support groups.

- Reassure her by consistently reminding her that you will be there for her, that you will get through it together, and that it will pass.
- Check out postpartum.net.

Take it seriously, take action, and you will get through it together.

> " Remember your wife has gone through a lot of changes. You'll find that she'll start crying and she won't know why. Just hold her hand and tell her it's going to be okay. She's going to be sore, tired, overwhelmed; she'll think she's ugly or a bad mom. And you're going to think you're a bad dad sometimes, too!"
>
> — Veteran Dad

ONLINE RESOURCES

postpartum.net
Online support, articles and links to other resources.

postpartumdads.org
Support for dads whose partners have postpartum depression or "baby blues".

tiny.cc/DepressionPregnancy
Depression during pregnancy and after the baby.

tiny.cc/PostPartum
Postpartum depression and depression in general. Leans towards treatment with drugs.

Romancing a New Mom

After two to three months your roller-coaster life with a newborn will probably be settling down. This is a time for you and mom to refocus on each other. Since she will likely be preoccupied with the baby, the ball is in your court to take the initiative on establishing the relationship you want for the next decade.

Understand that You are Starting Over

Re-kindling the romance in your relationship is a lot like starting on a fresh courtship. It can take time.

Communication Is Critical

Talking is how we sort out and resolve problems, and several months after the birth, the stack of issues can be high. Talking can also evolve into verbal foreplay… *sometimes*.

Tell Her Your Dream

And ask about hers. Talking together about your future, remembering your pre-baby past, and sharing your dreams brings the two of you closer.

Encourage and Respect Her as a Mom

Nothing, not even getting back into her favorite pre-baby jeans, will be as important to her self-esteem as the job she is doing as a mom.

Do Your Part as a Father

She is now viewing you as her baby's father. When she watches you giving him a bath or rocking him to sleep on your chest, she sees a happy baby and a **hot dad** (see "verbal foreplay" under Communication is Critical above!).

Get Out Together With Your Baby on Weekends

Go on a date with mom and your baby - to a sporting event, the zoo, or just out for a walk.

> " For our anniversary, I gave my wife a box with 5 date nights so we could be husband and wife again after the baby came. One was a bag of popcorn with a dollar so that I could run and get a Redbox movie. Another was two empty cups from her favorite ice cream shop. A third was a bottle of fake champagne so we could sit in the backyard and have it after the baby was asleep. It doesn't matter what it is, but if you do this, you have five boxed dates ready to go."
>
> — Veteran Dad

Give Her Time Alone

While with the baby she is on call for his slightest need or demand. This means she will need some time for herself. Make sure she gets it. If possible, get her out with her girlfriends.

Engage in Adult Conversation

Help break up her isolation by asking her about anything other than the baby (current events, her pre-baby interests, what's going on with friends, etc).

Help Her Re-Engage Her Mind

Encourage her to read a novel, go to a movie or take up a hobby; anything that broadens her horizons beyond the baby.

Eat Together

As simple as it sounds, it's a great way to begin reconnecting with your partner. Prepare a gourmet dinner together and start a tradition for your new family.

Exercise Together

A mom who gets regular exercise is a happier mom. Getting exercise together by walking (or jogging or bike riding) with your baby is a great idea.

Bring Out the List

Remember the list you made during her pregnancy, of things you like to do together? It's time to bring it out, pick one of the items and do it. Post the list on the refrigerator to remind you both that regular "mom and dad" time is essential.

> " It's the little things that are important, like when you walk into the house after work, always kiss her first and maybe give her some flowers. That will reassure her that she is every bit of a woman that she has ever been even though she is a mother."
>
> — Veteran Dad

SIX CHARACTERISTICS OF HAPPY PARENTS

Researchers found couples who successfully overcame the polarizing effects of a first baby shared six key characteristics:

1. Surrender individual goals and work together as a team.
2. Resolve differences about division of labor and argue constructively.
3. Keep common interests despite priorities that are branching off in different directions.
4. Understand their marriage will never be quite the same after the baby's arrival.
5. Continue communicating in a manner that sustains and supports the marriage.
6. Each handles frustration in a way that does not overstress their partner or their marriage.

Getting Your Love Life Back

Let's face it: as a new dad, pent up sexual frustration can make you come on too strong. The trouble is, your wife needs you to be patient and romance her first. Coming on too strong will be highly counterproductive.

Don't Push Her: When it comes to romance, applying too much pressure on your partner to get things back on track will backfire.

Cuddle: She has a lot of physical contact with a demanding baby and may not want any more at first. Take it slow and give her a foot rub, back rub, some hugs, and spoon.

Go to Bed Together: Just having a little window of private time goes a long way. You can use it to chat, snuggle, or whatever else feels right.

Schedule Dates: They don't always work due to changing priorities and intrusions, but if nothing is scheduled you may never get around to it. Take the initiative to schedule the dates and handle arrangements (sitter, etc.).

Sex in Six Weeks to Six Months

Most doctors say that six weeks after a normal vaginal delivery, she should be good to go. Actually, she'll be good to go when she is physically ready, and when she feels like it. That is, she is ready if she's feeling rested, good about her baby, good about her body, and good about you. This could take a while.

The New Rules of Foreplay: Quadruple your standard foreplay timeframe to give her plenty of time to warm up and push all thoughts of the baby out of her mind. Try a long massage. Start at her feet and slowly work your way up.

SIMPLE WAYS TO REMIND HER YOU LOVE HER

1. Quick phone calls: "Just wanted to hear your voice."
2. Email: "Had some good news and wanted you to be the first to know."
3. Love notes for her to find at home.
4. A quick neck rub in the morning.
5. Go for a walk and hold her hand.
6. When you come home from work, give her a kiss, then take the baby.
7. Buy her flowers.
8. Put up pictures of her and the baby around the house.

" If you ever want to have sex again with your wife, make sure she gets plenty of rest."

— Veteran Dad

Relearn What She Likes: Pregnancy and nursing may have changed your wife's hot spots. Go with what her body responds to, not with your old playbook.

Learn Bedroom Finesse – Maybe for the First Time: Most guys aren't exactly Don Juan in bed. If you want her to enjoy herself as much as possible, you may need to learn how to really turn her on. Men's magazines are full of advice and ads for better sex videos.

Get Away: An overnight trip + a romantic location not too far from home + a trusted babysitter = sexual nirvana. Make sure the sitter can reach you if need be. If mom's breastfeeding, don't forget the pump.

The First Time

Making love for the first time after having a baby is generally awkward, and often uncomfortable. It might be funny, but the odds are against it being hot. Make sure she's ready, rested, and relaxed. Tell her she looks beautiful. Start with a gentle massage, kissing and hugging. Most important, take your time and be gentle.

Talk it through beforehand. Let her know that you care, and want to know what she thinks will work best.

Make it a special event, a milestone for your new relationship as parents by doing it up right. If flowers were ever appropriate, this is the time.

Set the stage. Make sure the baby is handled, soft music, a candle and perhaps a little wine will help.

Lubrication often is necessary, keep some within reach.

Be careful around her breasts. They can be very tender from the baby's vigorous sucking.

Keep her comfortable. Go slow and use positions that let her control the action (mom on top).

Keep expectations low and be flexible; your objective should be basic lovemaking and nothing more.

If it becomes painful, of course, stop, and hold off until another day.

Consider non-coital alternatives, use your imaginations.

Make it an act of love, no matter what happens. End it on a high note.

> " This was my first experience as a married man with almost sex. As in, 'We almost had sex this morning.'"
> — Veteran Dad on the challenges your love life faces when being interrupted by a crying baby:

Mommyland

Mommyland is what we call the huge motherhood industrial complex that supports mothers and their babies. It consists of a $100 billion health care sector, lots of mom and parenting books and magazines, enormous websites, legions of mom bloggers, daytime talk and reality TV, Babies 'R' Us, Motherhood Maternity, Mommy & Me and more. Basically, it's the mom universe that organically forms overnight for each new mom-to-be.

It's a surreal, parallel world that creates whirlwinds that suck our new mom mates up like Dorothy in the Wizard of Oz, assimilates her into a new land and indoctrinates her on what to do and believe and how to behave as a mom. It hazes her as she runs the gauntlet of pregnancy and birth, and then keeps creating new demands on what it means to be a "good mother". Just saying.

Mommyland is fueled by a form of fusion; moms' hormonally supercharged buttons

coupled with their 85% discretionary purchasing power, which has every marketer in the country pushing them to make the "right" choices. It can be like never leaving high school.

Dads, unaware of the danger, watch in confused awe (especially when we walk into Babies 'R' Us), and then wake up one day to find we have been slowly transferred by osmosis one molecule at a time to Mommyland .

Dads in Mommyland

The institutions and marketing consortiums that represent the infrastructure of Mommyland unwittingly create an atmosphere that ignores you. It's as if dads don't exist, or if they do they are unnecessary baggage that mom is left to manage; almost like having a second child to deal with. They target your mate with a stream of negative messages about your potential as her baby's father. You will lag (that's normal), dads don't do near as much for their families (your job doesn't count), and you don't want to know how prevalent the trashing of dads is in their forums.

Dads are grunts; we can take anything, so the lack of respect for us is no big deal. But Mommyland has little respect for our relationship with our mate, the foundation for our new family, and acts to undermine it. That is a problem that needs to be fixed.

When Boot Camp for New Dads started, 66% of marriages went downhill after the baby arrived, the main complaint being dad didn't do enough. Two decades later, dads have doubled their contributions at home while maintaining a heavy workload, so our relationships have improved, right? Not exactly. Mommyland has seen to it that now 70% of working moms and 68% of moms staying home report being "resentful" of dad. Be careful this negativity does not turn into a self fulfilling prophecy for your new family.

The Dark Side of Mommyland

Mommyland is a cake walk for new dads compared to what it puts new moms through. It demands she become a Saint the moment the test turns positive and worry about the drink she had the week before. It is often a judgmental, compulsive, guilt ridden, even angry world where "mommy wars" - moms against moms - are regularly launched. What other moms think becomes the predominant factor in her choices.

Mommyland hazes new moms just as they are trying to get their mommy legs. It spends enormous energy telling moms-to-be everything that could possibly go wrong; *What To Expect*, the 500-page, month-by-month bible on your mate's night stand, should be re-titled *Everything You Could Possibly Worry About*.

It adds substantial stress to mom's lives, not to mention a whole lot more for moms to do, and as a result, 92% of working moms and 89% of those staying home report feeling overwhelmed. Not good for families.

> **"** Dads don't seem to get as obsessed about the baby as moms do. He's better at keeping things in perspective."
>
> — New Mom

New Moms Are the Heart of the Matter

In Boot Camp for New Dads, the veterans have always advised dads-to-be that supporting mom should be a core objective. Teaching them to understand and support their mates became our major priority. This included the challenges a first baby brings to mom's and dad's relationship.

But nobody was teaching mom how to understand and support dad and work together to strengthen their relationship. So on behalf of babies, dads and moms, we have launched New Moms Hearts and Minds Project (NewMomsProject.org). When new moms and dads understand and appreciate each other, they work together, do a better job for their baby, and are much happier. This is a great way to build a new family.

A few suggestions for re-romancing the new mom in your life:

Take the Initiative

Your baby is her priority, so relationship management is now all on you. She will think you can or should read her mind too. It is all normal. Take the initiative and talk to her. Make the list of things you like to do together to get out when your baby is six months.

> " I know we're supposed to let our husbands be involved and let him do things with the baby his way, but it's really, really hard!"
>
> — New Mom

TEN THINGS NEW MOMS NEED TO KNOW ABOUT NEW DADS

1. You have a lot of support; a dad-to-be has you.
2. Moms are the key to a new dad's success.
3. Expect he will do his part and he will.
4. Men thrive on respect, confidence and love.
5. Babies thrive on the difference dad brings.
6. With experience, confidence builds; our instincts kick in.
7. It's not about sex, it's about love.
8. OK – it's partly about sex.
9. If he brings his child into his world, you get balance in yours.
10. Become a team when the test turns positive.

Send mom-to-be over to NewMomsProject.org to find more info, including tips on how to support you.

Get Some Relationship Skills

While the mysteries of male-female relationships make our pre-baby life interesting, fun, and dramatic, for a team setting out on life's ultimate challenge - building a family - mysteries are not good. Making the transition from pre-baby couple to a family in which mom and dad still love each other is a huge challenge. You will need a strategy and the skills to make it happen. Check out the resources at DadsAdventure.com.

Take One for the Team

When that whirlwind from Mommyland arrives and inundates her with things to worry about and do, hold her tight, tell her she is going to be a great mom, and encourage her to tell you everything on her mind. Just listen. If she needs a virtual punching bag to exercise her hormonally-driven frustrations, you're it — take those hits with pride. Dads are grunts — we can take anything.

The goal of getting most of her back to form a solid cornerstone for your family is worth any investment.

> She used to be the one to take care of the relationship, but she's not going to be thinking of that now. So it's your job. It's going to be very different with the baby here and you need to rebuild things for the future."
>
> — Veteran Dad

YOUR RELATIONSHIP WILL BE REDEFINED

"The hardest part for me in supporting her, was the hormones going through her system in the first week, which will totally amaze you.

"At one point I looked at my wife and said I don't know who you are, I'm going to get calm for awhile, your mom's here and you're good.

"The baby was really, really good, but what no one ever tells you is that the first year, you're redefining your marriage. And, you wouldn't expect it because everybody talks about how joyful a time it is, and it is joyful, but it will challenge you.

"So, enjoy the time you have before the baby comes and really get to know your wife, and really remember those moments because you will be challenged."

— Veteran Dad

CHAPTER 5

Transforming Into A Dad

> **"**Step up and be there. And keep coming back. You're going to make mistakes – everybody does. You learn on the job."
>
> — Veteran Dad

Preparing to Become a Father

A Great Time to Become a Dad

You could not have picked a better or more challenging time to become a dad. Fatherhood is coming out of a century long slump, and the driving force is dads who simply want to provide their children the close bond they wish they had with their own father. The downside of fathers who were not part of their kid's lives is also very clear to us, and we are not about to let it happen to our kids, or to ourselves.

Dads today bring a strong commitment to raising children, and this in turn creates new respect for the importance of all fathers. It is also opening doors and creating opportunities for new fathers, as well as raising the bar for you regarding your involvement with your child. While our job today is tougher in some respects, the payoff in terms of being close to our kids is priceless, and it fuels our drive to get the job done.

How Do You Prepare?

Expecting moms are motivated by a baby growing inside them, major hormonal changes and decades of socialization, all while being supported by a committed network of mothers, medical services and the publishing industry; all you have is your expecting wife. If you are lucky, you have a friend who recently became a father that you can talk to. And if you are smart, you will talk to such friends and make new ones to find out what you are getting into. Other suggestions:

❑ Go to a childbirth and baby care class, and Boot Camp for New Dads (or other) if available.
❑ Read up; cruise your wife's books and make use of books and videos for fathers.
❑ Count on going through rough patches. If you don't, you are either very lucky or you are not trying hard enough.

PREPARE TO STAND YOUR GROUND

Make sure you and mom are clear on your plans for being an involved father. It's not uncommon for a new mom to be so immersed in the baby that she becomes a "gatekeeper" restricting dad's participation. If this happens, be patient and understanding, but make sure you are not pushed out of your child's life. Ditto with your mother-in-law, boss, and friends. Many men who worked hard to provide for their families have been surprised to find out down the road that they weren't really a part of their children's lives.

" Parenting – it's like a cult. You can't understand it until you're in it and you can't imagine things any other way."
— Veteran Dad

- ❏ Assess your feelings and work through them. Get past issues such as "not being ready to have a child," because they will preclude a focus on getting prepared.
- ❏ No matter your worries, be pro-active in getting ready. This will minimize worries.

A Process with Ups and Downs

Becoming a dad doesn't happen overnight. While the learning curve is sharp at first, it tapers off and extends for decades. You have a nine-month warm-up period, hell week lasts from one to three months, and then you'll find your groove. Becoming a dad is an intensely personal process that includes doubts and frustrations along with peak times when she smiles and you feel like a billion dollars. Focus on getting past those first months, and then work out a course for the long term.

Prepare for the Worst and the Best

Becoming a father can be very tough. We don't sugar coat it; we tell it like it is for a lot of men, which is how it might be for you. Or it might not. If you assume that all the hard stuff you hear or read about will happen to you, then you are getting it wrong. Nobody gets hit with all of it; just be ready for whatever comes your way, good or bad, because either way, you will want to make the best of it.

CONNECT WITH OTHER DADS

We can learn a great deal from each other. The problem is, for the most part, dads-to-be don't ask, and experienced fathers don't tell – unless asked. Break the ice and talk to other dads and request their suggestions and advice. They may be caught a little off guard because no one asked before, but it's a great way to both complement a man and learn from his experience.

" We were sitting around the fire at an Indian Princess campout and we started talking about our girls. I was relieved that my worries were minor compared to some of the guys, and inspired that no matter what they were dealing with, there was nothing they wouldn't do for their daughters."

— Veteran Dad

Common Fears and Concerns

After finding out you're going to be a dad, you may experience doubt, fear, second thoughts, even panic. No matter what's going on inside, you are far from alone. Much of it is mind games caused by rapid, fundamental change in your life. So if you find your emotions ranging from euphoria to dread, take a deep breath and remember it is normal. This will allow you to focus constructively on the real challenges you foresee. Note your concerns as a first step. At the risk of giving you more to worry about, here's a sample of some things soon-to-be fathers think about:

- What am I getting into?
- This was not my choice.
- I don't even like babies.
- I'm not ready.
  I won't be a good father.
- I'll throw up in the delivery room.
- I'll blow it as a birthing coach.
- I'll drop the baby.
- I'll lose a great life.
- Can she handle this?

- How much pain will she be in?
- What if there are complications?
- Will she ever get back to normal?
- Will she be a good mother?
- I can't afford a bigger house, another car.
- How much is this going to cost?

- I work 60 hours now/how can I pay the bills and spend the time with our baby?
- We barely make it now, and she wants to stay home.
- When will my sex life return?
- My mother-in-law is a nightmare.
- Is this baby really mine?
- I just want him to come out.
- I'll lose a great wife.

Your Life Will Change – But How?

We generally have a full life before our first baby comes along. Our careers are usually building or are already in full swing. We have fulfilling relationships with our mates, spending time together and sharing common interests. We have friends, hobbies, activities, or physical endeavors that fill up our days. In many cases, long work hours have already stretched our time to the limit. You will hear that your life as you know it is over. But what does this mean?

Fathers of toddlers will tell you they were surprised at how much work is involved. Becoming a dad means having more things to do than the time to do it. So while you work harder, you have to cut back on the things you now enjoy. You also have to make choices between competing priorities. You may want to take time off without pay when the baby comes, but then you wonder how you are going to pay for all of this. There has to be a reward for fatherhood, otherwise 40 million men in the U.S. wouldn't do it.

> " I'm concerned about how I'm going to meet my financial responsibility as the breadwinner of the family, and my moral responsibility as a father. I work long hours already. Now with the baby coming, I don't know how I'm going to find time to be a dad."
> — Rookie Dad

Babies Change Relationships, Many for the Better

New babies strengthen the love and respect of about one-third of new parents who together overcome the challenges and share the rewards of building a family. About half of couples find their relationship suffers; they were uninformed and unprepared for the impacts of a new baby, and when theirs arrived, they were unable to communicate and work out their issues.

No matter how much two people love each other, becoming a family can polarize you and your mate. Differences in values, backgrounds, personalities, and concerns sharpen as the demands of an infant press down on you. Nothing is more important to a child and his parents than their relationship, so a major investment in making yours work is warranted. Mom will be focused on the baby, so you need to be proactive. Set aside time to discuss priorities in raising your child, how you want to work together, and how you will handle the inevitable conflicts that arise.

How to Handle Sympathy Pains

If you experience unusual nausea, major weight gain, insomnia, or food cravings that mimic your mate's symptoms, it is likely that you are experiencing sympathy pains (couvade syndrome). While your friends may rag on you, the net result is you will likely be a better dad:

- Men who share symptoms with their mate report feeling close and connected to her and the baby, and that she appreciated his "sharing" her pregnancy.
- Couvade syndrome is now thought to be triggered by biochemical and hormonal changes in dads-to-be.
- Research shows that men who experience couvade are likely to spend more time caring for their babies.

Couvade syndrome starts at the end of the first trimester and ends with birth. If you experience couvade, take a positive view and remember all that will be left when your baby arrives is your pre-disposition to be a great dad. (P.S.: The record for men, is a beer belly that mimics mom's at 7 months.)

" I was born in South Central and when I was 2 years old, my dad collapsed and died. My mom was left with 5 kids in an area infested with gangs. One of my brothers is in prison, but I wanted to break the cycle.

"Fast forward and I'm now a social worker. My girlfriend and I were mad at each other (although we couldn't have been too mad because she was taking a pregnancy test). It came out positive. I was shocked. Mostly shocked because she got the test from the 99-cent Store and I didn't know they had them there, but I was shocked. I was sure it couldn't be accurate (it was from the 99-cent Store!), so she took 6 more. Still pregnant.

"My anxiety was really high – I'd never had a dad. Would I be a good dad? It had been so hard to find a role model around me.

"And that was the biggest impact of the Boot Camp for New Dads workshop. There's really no way to describe it; seeing average guys like me with their babies. They were doing it. All I know is that I'm trying to do it too."

— Veteran Dad

Research: Our Children Need Us to Be Men

We Have Come a Long Way Re: Our Babies

For two decades we have witnessed researchers' views of fathers evolve. They have observed their quarry – dads like us - up close and personal in our own natural habitat. Early on, many reported fathers were uninvolved with their babies and were of little value in comparison to moms. This didn't seem right, particularly as we walked our crying baby to sleep once again. Yeah, we struggled at times, but it seemed like no matter what we did, we were being judged based upon the worst among us.

Research Catches Up

Over the past decade the researchers have caught up with the tremendous changes driven by the many dads on the job. They have concluded that we are not only involved, as dads we can have unique and profoundly positive impacts upon our children, and we are endowed by nature to both defend our families from threats and cherish and care for our kids from birth. They are also pursuing the notion that, like moms, millenniums of evolution and socialization have a significant effect on how we act when we become fathers.

" I didn't give birth, I don't have boobs, but I have a lot to offer."

— Veteran Dad

Our Children Need Us

Research catalogued by the National Fatherhood Initiative indicates that children whose fathers are a consistent, positive force in their lives do better socially, intellectually, and on a broad range of other factors ranging from economic status in childhood to peer relationships in adolescence, to productivity as adults. Other research findings include:

- Children of involved fathers manage stress better during their school years and enjoy improved physical well being, perceptual abilities, positive relationships, self-control and ability to take the initiative.
- A close, warm relationship with our daughters strengthens their feeling of competence and sense of femininity.
- The love and care of mom and dad have an equal impact on their child's well-being, happiness and academic success.
- A father's love and care are the major factors in combating a child's problems with conduct, delinquency or substance abuse, and an involved father's children are less likely be subject to the breakup of their family, poverty, teen pregnancy, violence or abuse.

Not only are we hugely important to our children, we have a big job ahead of us.

> " When I walk in from work, she knows it's playtime."
> — Veteran Dad

They Need Us to Be Ourselves

Of all the powerful and complex dynamics in the circle of life, a father's critical role in teaching his baby to play has got to be one of the coolest. Research has found that despite the obvious advantages moms enjoy in terms of baby appeal, two-thirds of 6-month-old babies choose dad when it comes to playtime. Fathers, perhaps due in part to maturity issues, are naturally designed to be her perfect playmate. Tickling, flight lessons, peek-a-boo and wrestling all come naturally. Playing is also bonding at its finest. Dads elicit radiant smiles and infectious belly laughs, sometimes with just a wink. And finally, playing is your baby's main job: it teaches him how to laugh and take risks, it develops his motor skills and speeds the development of his brain and nervous system. It's a dirty job, but remember when you are crawling on the floor, barking like a dog as you chase him around, it's dad's job.

They Need Us to Be Men

There are times in our child's life when we really need to step up and it may come early:

- Premature babies make initial life as a parent very stressful, and their smiles are delayed.
- A baby experiencing serious colic seems to go on a crying jag for the first three months.
- Babies born by caesarean incapacitate mom for weeks, leaving dad with a double load.
- Fathers of twins, triplets, etc., have to step up big time.

For those that do, the rewards come early too, as the research shows that by being there when their child really needed them, they formed a stronger connection and were more engaged in caring for their baby at 5 months and on.

Research: Biochemical Changes Help Drive Us Forward

More of Us Are Doing the Job and Have Raised the Bar for All Dads

The research is clear: we dads are getting what we want, we like it, and our children do too. A random survey conducted by the National Center of Education Statistics (NCES) of 6,300 fathers with 9-month-old babies at home found that:

- 80% rated themselves as "better than average or very good," 17% average; only 2% had some trouble as a father.
- 99% "agreed that fatherhood is a highly rewarding experience," with 84% saying they strongly agree and only 1% disagreed.
- 96% engaged in some type of physical play with their baby daily.
- 87% changed at least a few diapers each week.
- 90% take their baby with them on errands once or twice a week.
- 100% find holding and cuddling their child is fun, with 85% finding this to be the case all the time.

> " Hey guys, can we stop talking about MOM?
> I don't know about you guys but I'm riding an emotional roller coaster too!"
>
> — Rookie Dad

We Often Start Out Way Behind the Curve

The same NCES study, however, also found that at conception, 25% had not wanted the pregnancy to occur at all and another 19% did not feel ready and wished it had occurred later. Most came around as the stats above show, and they did by getting with the program early on: 95% saw the ultrasound, 97% felt their baby move, and 93% attended the birth. Participation in Boot Camp for New Dads is also expanding, which is a good thing because expectations of new fathers, and particularly our expectations of ourselves, is growing too. In essence, we have a lot more ground to cover than our dads had to cover, between the time we hear "I'm pregnant!" and the time our baby is born.

Biochemical Changes Help Drive Us Forward

Hormones have gotten a bum rap due to their impacts upon women, but they serve a purpose, and research indicates we experience some changes as well in the weeks before and after the birth. And like boosting our testosterone and endorphins with exercise, we can help them kick in and harness their power to enhance our experience and capabilities as fathers. Research has found:

- Cortisol, the stress hormone, doubles in the three weeks before birth. It intensifies our feelings and response to our baby's cries, and also fuels our fight-or-flight impulse, which explains our heightened protective instinct.
- Prolactin, increases 20% in the weeks before birth, which likely enhances our instincts to care for our baby.

- Testosterone drops 33% in the three weeks after birth, and bounces back to normal at 4-7 weeks. Beyond temporarily diminishing our sex drive, this enables a strong emotional focus on our baby during this prime bonding period.

Apparently we are biologically predisposed to care for our child as well as pull him from a burning building. The key to taking advantage is to stay close to mom during pregnancy (which triggers our changes), and then take advantage of them by quickly getting hands-on in caring for our baby. In fact, starting with holding our baby for the first time, most fathers have an intuitive feeling that something in them has changed, and this new research validates decades of such feelings.

Months Surrounding Birth Provide Us a Window of Opportunity

Princeton's Center for Research on Child-Wellbeing found that virtually all new dads want to be good fathers, and the months surrounding the child's birth is a window of opportunity during which fathers are most receptive to support and change. This dovetails with the new research above documenting our biological drivers during this period, and helps explain the success of Boot Camp for New Dads, which reaches men early and provides them the orientation that enables them to "hit the ground crawling" when their child arrives.

> " Being a dad is pretty cool. The first couple of months were difficult, but when she looks across the room and finds me, it's just cool."
>
> – Veteran Dad

We Have Unique and Profound Impacts

Kyle Pruett, MD, author of *Fatherneed* (2000), explains "why a father has so powerful an influence on the kind of person his child eventually becomes." In his first chapter, "Fathers Do Not Mother," a key conclusion was that a father and his infant develop an enhanced relationship through interactions that occur between them "in the absence of the mother." This one-on-one time is when dads develop a broad range of skills for engaging their infants, who in turn benefit from richer social and exploratory behavior, smile more frequently and more often present toys to their dads.

> " If you're wondering how your life changes, there's only one word for it. Completely."
>
> – Veteran Dad

Strategies For When Your Time is Short

Parenthood often comes at a time in a man's life when he has to work 60-hour weeks, and some dads believe they can make up for lost time later. The truth is, you can't. The first three years of your child's life are the most vital in shaping who he will become later in life. You will never have other opportunities like those when your child is an infant, so make sure that you do spend time — even if it's just a couple of hours a week — alone with your baby now.

Dealing with Economic Realities

Of course, today's economic realities create difficult circumstances. Many careers demand long work hours, your new baby will add to your financial requirements, and your mate is going to be out of commission as an income generator for at least a little while. Taking a month off when your baby is born may be as much an option as going to the moon. Even making sure you're available for the birth itself may be difficult.

> " I'm nervous about going back to work and then coming home, having a million things to do, taking care of the baby, taking care of my wife, fixing things around the house, making food, and all the extra things I'll have to do, and trying to figure out what's most important."
> — Veteran Dad

Many veterans faced such circumstances, and you can learn from their ideas:

- Do everything you can to assure you are there for the birth. Missing the birth will be the biggest regret that you have.
- Change that first diaper. Make the time you do have count as much as possible. Set the tone that you are here to be a player and get involved early.
- Strive for solutions that enable you to spend time with your child. Be creative. Figure out how to work from home; even once a week is better than nothing.
- Play a strong role in providing emotional support for mom (such as calling her from work and emailing her; ask how she is doing or let her know how proud you are of her).
- When you are home, spend time alone with your baby. Don't let your limited experience as a caregiver interfere. Send mom out with some friends and just do it.
- If you simply have no choice, do not allow yourself to feel diminished because you can't spend lots of time with your new child. Your work and income is your family's lifeline.

It will probably be an ongoing challenge for you and your family. Two-thirds of fathers report that they would spend more time at home with their children if they were financially able to do so.

> " I usually take over when I get home from work, but I'm tired and it takes a lot of patience not to become short-tempered with the baby."
> — Veteran Dad

When You Spend a Lot of Time Away from Home

Spending time away from your little one can be tough, especially when you're talking a week or even a month at a time. Travel for long periods, as for military personnel, can be depressing. It's important to stay focused on why we work in the first place – to provide for our families. Even if your involvement with your child is minimal, it's important to make sure that involvement is as meaningful as possible:

- Play with your baby before you leave in the morning and just after you get home. Many dads report that their babies sleep longer if they play with them at night.
- Keep his picture where you see it often, and keep him in mind while you're on the road.
- Call mom often and get the lowdown on junior's antics and accomplishments for the day.
- Enlist mom, who can send you pictures and recordings and hold the phone to your baby's ear so you can talk to him, or show him his daddy on a cell phone picture.
- Get creative. A young father recently deployed to Iraq tape recorded a dozen nursery rhymes that his wife plays for their baby so that he will recognize dad's voice when he gets back home.

Also, remember the pioneering dads of a decade ago who had the courage to tell their boss they were going to cut back on their time in the office to spend more time at home; they opened a door for the rest of us.

INVOLVEMENT & BALANCE

WORK OPTIONS	IMPLICATIONS & IDEAS	WHAT IT MEANS TO YOUR FAMILY
Workaholic, Road Warrior, Deployed	The reality may be you need to work more to pay the bills, or meet essential career demands or military obligations. If you make your time at home with your family count, this can work for a couple of years. Make sure working more is not just an excuse to get away from the stress at home.	You are providing essential economic support, especially if it allows mom to stay home, but your family will mostly be without the benefit of a dad. You will miss out as well, so you will need an exit strategy. See on page 84 for ideas on how to make your time away from home count too.
Cut Back On Long Hours or Work Partly From Home	Some employers are responding with flexible schedules and telecommuting to fathers' desires to spend time with their children. You will need to request or even push for these options. Many fathers also find they are able to work more efficiently in order to spend more time at home.	Work flexibility and working fewer nights and weekends will allow you many more opportunities to interact with your child and support mom. Working at home requires discipline on your part, and it is hard to actually care for a child when doing so, but you get to be there for your family.
Find Less Demanding Job	Backing off on your career aspirations is a sacrifice, but finding another job with fewer hours, perhaps in the same company, may be your best option. In addition to time, stress is also a factor as we tend to bring it home, so reducing stress is as important as reducing work hours.	This likely involves a decrease in pay as well as a serious increase in your fulfillment as a father. Research is clear on the benefits babies receive from having dad around, and it brings much appreciated balance to mom's life as well. Start by talking with her about the trade-offs.
Reduce Commute Time	Moving closer to work or finding a job closer to home will result in less time on the road and more time with your family. Easier said than done of course, but check out the possibilities; a family-friendly neighborhood or even a less demanding job may also be part of the deal.	The time you save can be considerable, and it is prime time in the morning and early evening when your child is awake and ready to go. The commitment it takes to make these kinds of changes reflects a real dad who gets it and starts off in a strong position to make the most of it.
Set Up Business At Home	It involves risks, but if successful, it is a great combination of a good income, no commute and a flexible schedule that enables you to optimize your time on the home front. It requires personal discipline and practical steps like a separate work area, but it can bring balance to your new life.	A great option if you can pull it off, as you pay the bills and are able to fully participate in your children's upbringing. There are business risks, but overhead is low and this is a great way to go when the kids are young. Be careful that business stress does not diminish you as a dad.
Work Part Time	Most new families have two working parents and in many mom is a major income generator. This enables more men to work part time and become the major care giver to their babies supported by part-time day care. A part-time job can also counteract the boredom inherent in full time baby care.	The alternative is two parents working full time, which tends to be very stressful for new families. Part time work can involve cutting down on hours at your current job, starting a home-based business, or finding a part time job. Work out the best possible arrangement with mom.
Be A Stay At Home Dad	Staying at home to raise your child may be one of the most rewarding things you ever do. It also may not work for you, especially if your motivation is to get out of a lousy job. Don't doubt your ability though: 150,000 dads stayed home in 2004 and many more would join them if they could.	You will be the most important influence in your child's life. Traditional norms of dad as breadwinner are dissipating along with social pressures stay-at-home dads experience. Take a professional approach to make the most of this opportunity or you may find it boring and demeaning.

The Impact of Fatherhood on Men

A Glimpse of Your Future

So what is it like to be a father? At our workshops, "veteran" dads bring and care for their several month old babies and explain what they have learned. The rookies see men with a calm confidence and sense of pride and purpose that is very reassuring. They have gotten through the tough early months, their babies now smile at them; these are upbeat fathers, men on a mission of creating their own family with mom.

You Will Transform into Dad

Over time we gradually develop a new, stronger sense of ourselves as fathers. As we learn to meet our baby's needs, we come to trust our instincts, just as moms do. As we become comfortable in raising our children and helping them learn new things, we develop an awareness of how important we are to them. While this transformation into a father occurs in the circumstances of our new lives, it ultimately takes place in the depths of our own minds. We start to feel like "dad" and build an extraordinary commitment to do our best for our child. It quickly becomes a big part of who we are, a new dimension that enlarges us, make us better men.

> " I fear that I might get too wrapped up in my work and career and not be there for my family. Not spending enough time to bond with my child is of great concern to me."
> — Rookie Dad

Your Child Offers You a Great Deal

Little can compare to your baby falling asleep in your arms, comforting an upset baby, or a toddler's delight over knocking down the block tower you helped him build. No matter what happens in the rest of our life, we are always special to our child. We can tell you that as a rich relationship with your child develops, you will experience a sense of manhood that fills your heart and soul and fulfills the core of your being. It will have a broad, pervasive impact upon you that gives real and deep meaning to your life.

Opportunity to Show What We Are Made Of

Becoming enmeshed in caring for a baby on turf owned by women (for millenniums) can feel emasculating at first, but we end up carving out our turf and figuring out how to do it our own way. We also learn taking care of a sick baby through the night is not for wimps, and that protecting and providing for a family requires a great deal of strength. Raising children brings out the best in us and spurs us to mature and excel as human beings. We develop an extraordinary commitment to our child and family and become men in the finest sense of the term.

When You Get Overwhelmed or Close to It

If you find the whole scene seriously getting to you, do something about it:

- **Try to get enough sleep.** Grab a nap when possible – a little sleep can go a long way.
- **Be realistic.** The demands of fatherhood can easily push you past your limits, and you can't do everything. Let yourself off the hook once in a while and de-stress.
- **Take things gradually.** Give yourself time to warm up to the big changes you are facing.
- **Share your feelings** with your partner. Let her help you sort them out.
- **Laugh.** You can always find something funny in any situation if you try. And sometimes the toughest things you go through are also the most amusing in retrospect.
- **Do something creative** to break out of the doldrums. Get out the camera and get some pictures of your new family developed and framed and put them up around the house.

> " The best advice I can give you is to keep communication open and try to offer each other breaks if at all possible."
>
> – Veteran Dad

- **Stay involved.** When exhaustion and frustration set in, everything in you wants to back off. You need to do the opposite. When you feel most like tuning out, push yourself to take the baby for a walk or give your partner a back rub. Soon you will find that overcoming your own resistance becomes easier and more gratifying.
- **Get away.** Spend time together on a date or even overnight with your mate.

Kick Back with Your Friends

Standard procedure for new fathers is to give up the few friends we have (a) because they foster anti-social behavior and (b) they are not interested in the color of our baby's poop. The bottom line is that we get isolated and cooped up just when we need to get out and de-stress. Your buddies provide balance in your life, especially when the pressure builds. So if you are feeling it, for the sake of your family, call up your friends and go out and have a beer. Review the sports section first so you have something to talk about besides the baby. It works a lot better if they have babies or kids themselves, as a little appreciation of your circumstances and semi-heroic efforts can do wonders for your attitude.

> " I felt pressured to always be there for my new family and play Superdad, never thinking that I needed time every once in a while to recuperate and refuel my daddy tank."
>
> — Veteran Dad

Connect with Other Dads

Take a page out of the new mom's playbook and network with the dads you know and connect with some new ones. Although they are a good bet, don't limit yourself to the mates of new moms your wife met in your childbirth class. Try your own father — you may be surprised by how much you have in common. Take your baby to go see your brother, or ask the guy down the hall at work or the one sitting next to you on the plane about their kids.

Getting together with other dads can quickly put you back on solid ground with a fresh head of steam. The veterans who do this uniformly report it to be both reassuring and motivating. If someone gushes about how wonderful everything has been since his baby's birth, explain the rules: points are only awarded for get-it-off-your-chest gripes and screw ups, and worst case scenarios win.

Dads Can Get Depressed Too

It can get you down too — at least 30% of new fathers experience significant depression due to all the stress they face and the enormity, speed and velocity of the changes occurring in their lives. If this happens to you, recognize it for what it is, understand it is normal, and deal with it constructively. Keep in mind that worrying about responsibility means you are on the job, and take comfort in the fact that men who do their job as fathers end up happier, healthier and more self respecting. Talk to your physician or another professional to make sure you get it handled.

How to Transform into a Dad

Any major challenge you take on in life – and no other can be more profound than fatherhood – warrants planning, preparing and improving as you go, and this page will enable you to get it done. It will help you not just survive, but thrive as a dad by facilitating your preparation of a game plan that you can adjust as you gain experience and your child grows.

1. Inventory Your Concerns as a Dad-To-Be

Review the list of common concerns of dads-to-be *on page 78* and check off or add those that pertain to you. Then note the three most important ones (the rest fall under a basic rule for new fathers: don't sweat the small stuff):

_____

_____

_____

2. Take Stock of Your Attributes as a Dad

Every man brings strengths and weaknesses to fatherhood, and an assessment of your "dad attributes" before your child arrives sure beats discovering your weaknesses the hard way down the road. Consider how you stack up on:
- Patience
- Selflessness (i.e., not selfish)
- Income production
- Building relationships
- Playfulness (i.e., never growing up)
- Time for your family
- Collaboration (with mom)
- Bad habits (tobacco, alcohol, drugs)
- Courage & perseverance

Consider your weaknesses and how you can overcome them. If you have a habit incompatible with being a dad, plan on dealing with it. Consider your strengths and how you can use them. If you have a good amount of time or flexibility to be with your child, what will you do with her? Taking note and strategizing early on will enable you to get a handle on any challenge and deal with it constructively.

3. Set Some Goals

Most moms are physically, emotionally and socially driven to make sacrifices from the moment the pregnancy test turns positive, and then are surrounded by mom mentors who show them the way. We dads are left to our own motivations and devices. Since we are on our own, defining our goals for our own fatherhood is essential; otherwise, we run the risk of getting caught up in the initial turbulence and letting circumstance chart our course. Use the tool on the following page to think through your initial goals as a new father and then track how you do.

> Just get into it from the beginning. Don't worry about doing it wrong, don't worry about doing it perfectly. As long as you get in there from the beginning and keep at it, it'll pay off huge dividends with your wife. Because she'll know she'll have someone there with her all the time who can take care of the baby if she's too tired. Don't be scared you're going to mess up, everyone does. Just get in there from the beginning and you'll be good to go."
>
> – Veteran Dad

4. Strategize on Re-Balancing Your Life

Research has found 75% of fathers want more time with their children. Start early on adjusting to the needs and your desires for your new family, especially if you have opportunities now that are unlikely to come along in the future. See *Work Balance Options on page 86*. Deal constructively with finances, income, career paths, one or two paychecks, etc. and if there are no short-term solutions, strategize and set goals for resolving them in the future.

5. Track Your Transformation

You are in the midst of a personal transformation that will profoundly change you. *A New Father's Transformation Milestones page 93* describes six stages through which all new fathers must pass to become a real dad. Check them out, add your own goals under "What to Shoot For," and note your progress over the first year.

6. Conduct Periodic Status Checks

A status check on your progress as a father will boost your confidence and provide a basis for adjusting your goals and strategies. Start with one coinciding with your baby's 6-week check-up and then do one quarterly for the first year.

7. Plan Your First Adventure With Your Child

Actually, make a list of the adventures you want with your child and another on what you would like to teach her (start with the form on the next page). This will set your sights beyond the drudgery to the nirvana of raising a child.

YOU ARE CHANGING THE WORLD

By doing your best as a dad, you will be on the front lines of a renaissance in fatherhood in America. You are improving the world for all children, including your own, by setting an example for the fathers who follow you.

> You get a lot of messages that women have maternal instincts and you kind of get the message that they're the only ones that do. But the fact is that dads have instincts too and I think that as long as you follow that I don't think you make too many bad choices."
>
> — Veteran Dad

My Goals As A Father

What Kind of Father Do I Want to Be?

A great question to ask. Start by thinking of your own father or a man who served in this role, and then ask yourself some questions. Here are some to get you started:

- What did he do best as a father?
- What would you do differently?
- What did you learn from him that you want to pass on to your children?
- Are there other fathers (or friends) who you want to emulate?
- Do you feel good about becoming a father?
- What concerns do you have?
- What values and attributes do you want to pass on to your children?
- What are your strengths and weaknesses for being a father?
- What kind of relationship do you want with your child?
- What do you want to do together as he grows?
- How do you want to work together with your mate to raise your child?

WHAT MY DAD DID RIGHT

"He worked really hard to support us. And he was always there for my sister and me."

"He was just all around great. He's going to be a great grandfather."

"He was always really support-ive of what we wanted to do."

Spell Out Your Goals

Goals give us a path to follow and stating them is the first step toward meeting them. Take an initial shot at listing your goals as a father and periodically revisit and update them to stay on track. (This is for you, not the baby book.)

VALUES I WANT TO TEACH MY CHILD

_____

_____

_____

_____

_____

HOW I WANT TO BE REMEMBERED AS A FATHER

_____

_____

_____

_____

_____

" My dad worked hard, but when he was home, he liked to be with me. I could always talk to him about stuff. I still can. I hope to raise my son the same way."

— Veteran Dad

A New Father's Transformation Milestones

	Milestones & Challenges	What To Shoot For
DEPLOY	Ready or not, "I'm pregnant!" is the kickoff! (44% of us say not). To become part of your child's life, you need to get ready before his birth. This includes getting in sync with your mate, dealing with your concerns, thinking through what kind of dad you want to be, etc.	Deploy means get organized and get ready: • Go to the doctor visits and ask questions • Help her through pregnancy and talk to her • Feel your baby kick and talk to him as well • Get comfortable with basic baby care • Prepare yourself to be her childbirth coach
DELIVER	When her labor kicks in, it is time to deliver. Coaching her through childbirth is intense and perhaps harrowing, but you will do it. Next, welcome your baby into the world! Then take your family home where you will need to seriously deliver for weeks on end.	Deliver means be ready and get it done: • Be her calm, reassuring birth coach • Make the birth special for mom and dad • Get hands-on in caring for your baby • Take care of mom; do whatever you can • Get sleep when you can; you will need it
DEPRIVED	With little sleep, a demanding baby and worn out mom, plan on hitting the wall when the adrenaline runs out after a few weeks. Even so, you still have to get up to care for your baby and then get up and go to work, with no end in sight through your bleary eyes.	Deprived is being exhausted and feeling the life you knew and loved is over: • Remember this phase will pass • Assess mom for baby blues (See on page 64) • Assess yourself (take 6 week checkup) • Focus on the basics; let the rest slide
DISCOVER	Hey, you've gotten the hang of taking care of your baby! And after 3 months, her crying cuts way back! And she smiles when she sees you! She's still lots of work, but you learned what works and are getting a second wind and a sense of control over your life.	Discovery means enlightenment: • Teach your baby to play peek-a-boo • Take her out on your own once a week • Think about future adventures together • Start romancing the new mom in your life • Consider the kind of father you want to be
DELIGHT	Now this is getting fun! He gets all excited when you walk in the room and he can roll over, laugh, learn to do tricks. You have a new bud (or budette)! This is where bonding with your baby can skyrocket and lock you into a strong connection for life. Ride this wave!	Delight means fun and fulfillment for you: • Teach your baby to do 3 things (to start) • Share the fun with mom • Fanaticize about family adventures • Make your early experience as a new father positive to build momentum for the future
DAD	A dad puts his child's needs before his own, protects her from all threats, looks forward to their future together and builds a new sense of pride, confidence and purpose. When tough, remember it is not just a learning curve, you are on a growth curve as a man.	Reflect on the kind of father you've become! Continue to do your best as a dad; the lifetime payback is enormous. Make the most of it as a family – with mom – and you will find new moms love their baby's new daddy. Welcome to the brotherhood of fatherhood!

Get Ahead of the Curve!

The peak moments of fatherhood occur when you engage your child in adventures you enjoy together. They learn a great deal from these experiences, you learn how important you are to them, and the connection you build lasts a lifetime. Making a list of ideas means you will never have to try and think of something to do, so check *Adventures for 0 to 3 Months on page 132* for ideas, brainstorm and add your own, and start checking them off. There is no better habit to develop as a dad.

Adventures We Can Have

- ☐ _____
- ☐ _____
- ☐ _____
- ☐ _____
- ☐ _____
- ☐ _____
- ☐ _____
- ☐ _____
- ☐ _____
- ☐ _____
- ☐ _____
- ☐ _____

What I Can Teach My Child

- ☐ _____
- ☐ _____
- ☐ _____
- ☐ _____
- ☐ _____
- ☐ _____
- ☐ _____
- ☐ _____
- ☐ _____
- ☐ _____
- ☐ _____
- ☐ _____

New Dad Status Check-Ups

Instructions: Jot down your thoughts and track your progress as you transform into a dad.

First Status Checkup Coinciding with 6-Week Baby Checkup

Most new dads hit bottom around 6 weeks, so this is a good time to take stock of your progress. The initial excitement, attention and help are gone, replaced by exhaustion, frustration and ambivalence about having a baby, a mate who is in worse shape, and an incessantly demanding infant who may be screaming regularly with colic. Your work suffers, your sex life is history, exercise and time for yourself are rare, and there is no end in sight to your new life of drudgery and servitude (when it is time to vent, you want to get it all out). Take comfort in that you're halfway through the 3-month hump, after which babies quit crying so much and start sleeping longer.

Do Status Check Every Quarter for First Year

It is easy to lose perspective. Asking yourself some basic questions can help you get a grip on what is happening and clarify how you are doing as a father. There are no right or wrong answers:

YOUR BABY

- How do you feel about your baby?
- What were some of the best times you have had?
- What frustrates you about your child?
- Are you confident and capable in caring for your baby?
- How much time have you spent with your baby this week?
- What would you like to do better?

YOUR MATE

- Have your feelings about your wife changed?
- How about her feelings towards you?
- Are you working together as partners?
- Is the romance returning?
- How do you feel about her as a mom?
- What would you like to do better with her?

YOURSELF

- How are you feeling? Have you changed?
- What things do you like about being a father?
  What do you dislike?
- Are you satisfied with the job you are doing?
- Are you angry? Does your anger get in the way?
- Are you depressed? If so, are you getting it handled?
- What would you like to do better?

DATE: _____

Your Baby

_____

_____

_____

Your Mate

_____

_____

_____

_____

Yourself

_____

_____

_____

CHAPTER 6

Keeping Baby Safe And Healthy

" We let the dogs be loud and didn't tell them not to bark when she was pregnant, so when the baby was born, she was used to it."
— Veteran Dad

Keeping Your Baby Safe

Nothing's worse than seeing your child hurt and knowing you could have prevented it. So after he arrives, keep your protective instincts alert and operational. To help them fully kick in, take a first aid class oriented toward children and buy a first aid kit.

Dad Safety – The First Line of Defense

Basic male behavior can lean more toward the risk-taking macho variety than the assessing hazards and limiting risk type. Many men find, however, that once the baby is born (and even before), they begin to reevaluate hobbies (sky dive much?) and habits (how fast do you drive?). Why? You are the only dad she has, and it's in her best interest that you stick around for a while.

Some Things to Keep in Mind

- **Smoking -** Unlike you, your baby can't move out of harm's way. When you smoke around him, he gets even more of a hit than you do.
- **Toxins** – Including paints, lacquers (even nail polish and remover), and insecticides. Do not use them indoors or in the vicinity of your baby. A newborn's immune system is not fully developed, and these substances can be harmful even in small doses.
- **Pockets** – Empty your pockets before handling your baby. Things can fall out of your pockets without you even noticing and even swallowing a single penny might require your baby to go through surgery.
- **Sun Protection** – Because your baby has sensitive skin, it's important to avoid using sunscreen until she's 6-months old. Use other methods of keeping her out of the sun, like a baby-seat canopy. If you're taking a stroller walk, and the sun is in her face, just hang a light blanket over the stroller's canopy to shield her.
- **Water and Bathing** – Children under 1 year old drown most commonly in bathtubs, buckets, and toilets. In fact, your baby can drown in as little as two inches of water. You should never stray more than an arm's length from your baby while she's bathing.

- **Salt and Honey** – There are several food items that you should definitely avoid. Although you cannot keep sodium out of the baby's food, excess salt is detrimental to her kidneys and blood pressure. And up until a baby turns one, you should NEVER feed honey to a baby. Honey can cause infant botulism, which could lead to death.

THE SLIDE-AND-HIDE TECHNIQUE

Used toilet-paper tubes make superb measuring devices. If an object can slide down the tube, it can also slide down your baby's breathing passage. Don't let your baby fall prey to asphyxiation or choking.

> " I used to smoke two packs a day. When my baby was born, I walked out of the hospital and threw the cigarettes away. Every time I wanted to smoke, I would pick my daughter up and look into her eyes."
>
> – Veteran Dad

Baby Proofing – Things that Should be Done Before the Baby Arrives

- Set the water heater to 120°F to avoid scalding.
- Check smoke detectors and install them where needed.
- Get a fire extinguisher. If you already have one, make sure that it has recently been inspected.
- Cover radiators/space heaters.
- Bolt bookshelves and other tall cabinets to walls.
- Post emergency phone numbers (pediatrician, poison control center, etc.) near the phone. Or program them into the phone's speed dial.

Adopt a "Baby's-Eye" View

Even after you've baby-proofed, you should be continually assessing the safety of your baby's environment. One way is to get down to his level and look around. Is the surface he's lying on secure? Are there small objects around him that could get into his mouth? Sharp objects he can grab? Try crawling around and see if your knees discover any "unwanted" items and you'll see what the baby might run into as well.

" Get on your belly and crawl around. You'll be amazed at what you see."

— Veteran Dad

PREVENT FALLING

Make no mistake, your baby starts life with an underdeveloped sense of height and the injuries caused by falling. Here are precautions you can take:

- Close and lock (with as high a latch as possible) all doors at the top and bottom of staircases. If you have no staircase doors, install hardware-mounted safety gates at the top and bottom of the stairs; spring-mounted gates are not advised. If your stair rails are less than 3" apart, install mesh or plexiglass to block the openings.
- Never put baby seats on high surfaces.
- Put stick-on padding on the corners of tables.
- Use baby equipment with wide, sturdy bases.
- Secure or remove loose rugs.
- Install baby-proof latches on windows.
- Install baby protection on all kitchen drawers and cabinets to keep babies and toddlers from opening.

When to Baby Proof: Stay Ahead of the Curve

		3 MONTHS	6 MONTHS	9 MONTHS	ONE YEAR
	HEIGHT	Arms length up from the ground, or anywhere he can reach	May be sitting up – 1 ½ feet off the ground	May be standing against furniture – 2 to 2½ feet off the ground	Fully standing, on tip toes and fully reaching – over 3 feet off the ground
	WHAT CAN HE DO?	Grabbing – Anything within reach of his grubby little hands will get picked up and go into his mouth	Mobility – By scooting or rolling he can now get to even more dangerous stuff	Crawling – More prone to falling injuries as he is even more mobile and begins to experiment with walking	Walking and reaching – He's now a foot taller (then when he only crawled)
	WHAT TO LOOK FOR	• Cords/curtains • Sharp or small objects • Anything that can be pulled	• Electrical outlets and plugs • Anything that can be pulled down	• Stairs • Table corners • Drawers and cabinets • Toilets	• Everything
ACTIONS TO TAKE IN THE …	**BATHROOM**	• Keep baby out of arms reach of (nearly) everything	• Install toilet guard • Put non-slip mat in the tub • Install cabinet locks • Keep electric items (hair dryers, etc.) put away when not in use	• Install knob covers on bath • Put non-slip mat on outside of tub • Always keep tub empty of water	• Consider keeping baby out with a gate (at this age, there's just too much he can get into in there when not supervised)
	BEDROOMS	• Wrap up curtains and cords (pay attention to any near baby's crib) • Keep fluffy blankets, pillows, or stuffed animals out of crib	• Remove mobiles or hanging toys from crib (by five months) • Ensure crib is at least two feet from windows • Cover outlets, secure cords	• Ensure toy chest lid stays up when opened • Be aware of things that can be climbed on (rocking chair, open dresser drawers, etc.)	• Keep changing table items away from edge of table
	KITCHEN	• Ensure knives are secured • Wrap up curtains and cords	• Keep high chair away from walls (strong kicks against wall can knock the chair over) • Use unbreakable plates and dishes	• Install cabinet locks • Install oven lock and stove knob covers • Keep mouse and insect traps in inaccessible places	• Use back burners when cooking • Keep magnets out of reach • Lock dishwasher • Keep pet dishes in separate, locked room
	LIVING ROOM	• Remove all small objects (change, pens, hair clips, etc.) • Wrap up curtains and cords • Remove plants or put out of reach	• Secure fireplace screen and tools • Cover exposed outlets and secure exposed cords • Ensure lamps, TV, etc. can't be pulled down by cords	• Pad table corners and fireplace hearth • Move furniture away from windows • Put gates between rooms and at the top/ bottom of stairs	• Ensure nothing is low enough for him to reach and pull down • Put decals (at his height) on sliding doors

Preparing for Emergencies

When to Call 911
- Your child is not breathing or has difficulty such as breathing very rapidly
- He or she is unconsciousness
- Has been injured in or by a moving vehicle
- Serious wound or fractured bone
- Serious bleeding or severe burns
- Experiencing a seizure
- Choking on something you cannot help him expel
- A deformity of the skull, possible skull fracture
- Bleeding or clear fluid from the nose, ear, or mouth
- Has fallen more than 5 feet onto a hard surface
- Experiencing a condition you feel is life or limb threatening

Call 911 or yell for someone else to do so. Push the speakerphone button on your phone so you can hear instructions while you treat your child.

When to Go to the ER
- Evaluate a head injury
- X-Ray a possible broken bone
- A cut that may need stitches
- High fever or other serious illness
- Any condition that you feel may need emergent care

You can also call your doctor or nurse hotline for advice; they may save you a costly emergency room visit.

> " You're the protector of your child. Take an infant/CPR/choking class. You want to be the dad who saves your child, not the one running around who's screaming for help."
> — Veteran Dad

PRODUCT SAFETY
US Consumer Product Safety Commission
tiny.cc/ChildRecalls
Baby product recalls - great for checking second hand equipment.
KidSource.com/CPSC/ safety_tips.html
Tips on making your baby products safe.
tiny.cc/ChoosingSafeProducts
Advice on choosing safe products.

Poison Control Center 1-800 222-1222
Call 800-222-1222 if you suspect your baby has ingested a toxic substance. Call before symptoms develop and even if you just have a question about poisons. They will ask what was ingested (see the label), an estimate of how much, and when it happened. The Center will tell you what to do.

Keep First Aid Kit Handy
Keep a first aid kit at home and each car that includes the following items for a baby:
- ❑ Nonstick sterile pads to stop bleeding or cover wounds
- ❑ Adhesive bandages of different sizes
- ❑ Liquid soap/sanitizer (clean minor cuts and scrapes)
- ❑ Eye wash solution to flush eyes
- ❑ Thermometer to diagnose fevers

- ❑ Pain/fever reducers with baby dosages
- ❑ Antibiotic ointment (prevents infection)
- ❑ Burn ointment to soothe and protect skin after minor burns
- ❑ Ipecac (if advised by Poison Control Center)
- ❑ Gauze bandage roll and adhesive tape
- ❑ Small "ace" bandage
- ❑ A guidebook on first aid for children
- ❑ Instant cold pack to reduce swelling from bumps, etc.

If Going to the Great Outdoors Add

- ❑ SPF 15+ sunscreen; use only on babies older than six months
- ❑ Multi-tool knife with tweezers to remove splinters, ticks
- ❑ Hydrocortisone cream for insect bites, rashes, etc.
- ❑ Insect repellent for babies
- ❑ Snake bite kit (just kidding, mom, it's for dad.)

“ He fell and cut the inside of his lip and there was blood all over his face. But you have to be calm, because if you start to freak, mom starts to freak more. She's already on the edge and has the car started, ready to go to the hospital."

— Veteran Dad

HEAD INJURIES REQUIRE EXTRA VIGILANCE

Head bonks are common among babies due to the high proportion of their body weight in their heads. Falls are the main cause, so be watchful and protective as a general rule and avoid tossing your child in the air. If he does hurt his head, you will need to determine how serious it is and how to respond. The scalp is rich with blood vessels, so even a minor cut there can bleed profusely. Even if he appears OK, he may have an internal injury that can be very serious.

If it is obviously serious, call 911. If he won't stop crying, vomits multiple times, indicates unusual weakness or has pupils of unequal size or crossed eyes, take him to the ER. If no injury is evident but he fell from a significant height or was hit with significant force, call his doctor or nurse line for advice and direction; he may have suffered a concussion.

Infant CPR & Choking Basics

Learn CPR

Mickey Eisenberg, M.D.'s LearnCPR.org offers basic infant CPR and choking instructions in 30-40 second videos and the simple directions on this card (both available in 7 languages). You can easily download the videos to your computer to review with the instructions below and keep readily accessible. Learn CPR stresses that this cannot replace real CPR or first aid training and recommends attending a course in your community offered by the American Heart Association (call 1-800-AHA-USA1), the American Red Cross and many local fire departments.

FIRST AID FOR CHOKING INFANTS

1. Can your infant cry or cough?

If not, proceed to next step.

2. Give 5 back blows

3. Give 5 chest thrusts

4. Repeat steps 2 & 3

Repeat above until effective or the infant becomes unconscious. If the infant becomes unresponsive, perform CPR- if you see an object in the throat or mouth, remove it.

CPR FOR INFANTS

If alone with the infant give 2 minutes of CPR before calling 911, otherwise direct someone to call 911 immediately.

1. Shout and Tap

Shout and gently tap the child on the shoulder. If there is no response, and is not breathing or not breathing normally, position the infant on his or her back and begin CPR.

2. Give 30 Compressions

Give 30 gentle chest compressions at the rate of 100 per minute. Use two or three fingers in the center of the chest just below the nipples. Press down approximately 1½ inches.

3. Open the Airway

Open the airway using a head tilt lifting of chin. Do not tilt the head too far back.

4. Give Two Gentle Breaths

If the baby is NOT breathing or not breathing normally, give 2 gentle breaths. Cover the baby's mouth and nose with your mouth. Each breath should be 1 second long. You should see the baby's chest rise with each breath. Keep giving compressions and breaths until help arrives.

Introducing Pets to Your Baby

Dogs

Introducing your new baby to your dog is almost like bringing a baby home to a sibling; if handled incorrectly it can cause rivalry and hurt feelings. By taking a few simple precautions, though, your dog and baby should eventually become the best of friends.

- If you're going to take your dog to an obedience class, do it before the baby arrives, since you won't have the time after baby comes home. If your dog doesn't know basic commands then you might want to seriously consider classes.
- Any changes to the house rules need to be made before the baby arrives. You don't want your dog to associate the baby with her prohibition from sleeping in your bed.
- Have a vet check for parasites or other health concerns four to five months before the baby is born.
- Introduce your dog to baby blankets, lotions, rattles and toys before the baby comes home.
- To get your dog used to the baby's scent you can send home a blanket or gown from the hospital that the baby has been wrapped in.
- Have someone other than mom carry the baby inside the house for the first time. This will allow mom to greet the dog and may cut down on jealousy the dog feels later on over mom's attention to the baby.
- Try not to scold the dog while holding the baby, so that the dog doesn't connect the baby with discipline.
- Use positive reinforcement as much as possible (a treat or a hug), and reassure the dog whenever the baby cries.
- Make sure you still spend one-on-one time with your dog (during baby naps, or on walks).
- It might be a while until your dog is fully relaxed around the baby, so just be patient.

BREEDS OF CONCERN

Un-neutered male dogs and dogs trained or bred to be aggressive are not safe around children. Pit bulls, chows and rottweilers often fit this description. As a parent, it is now your responsibility to be honest about how your dog has been raised and whether it is safe around your child.

DO WHAT YOU NEED TO DO

If the dog shows aggression, or if you don't fully trust him, remember your priority is to protect your baby and the dog must go. Choosing between a new baby you barely know, and a dog that has been with you for years may be difficult, but think it through and do what you need to.

Cats

Scratches are a danger and cats are capable of jumping to get to an infant. Many cats find curling up and sleeping on a warm baby inviting, but this poses a risk of suffocation for the baby so extra vigilance is in order.

Exotics

If you own a large carnivorous reptile you probably don't need reminding that they can be dangerous. Anything that considers your infant a potential snack should either be removed from the home or monitored with extreme care.

- Smaller reptiles and amphibians can harbor dangerous bacterial diseases. Always wash thoroughly after handling them and before touching anything else.
- Birds may harbor parasites, and many people are allergic to feathers. Birds that are allowed to roam freely about the home pose obvious risks.

" It was my wife's dog before we got together, so when we brought the baby home, my wife went in one room with the dog and I took the baby in a different room. We let the dog see that my wife was ok and then did a slow introduction to the baby. Now the dog will bring the ball over to the baby and try to get her to throw it."

— Veteran Dad

TIPS AND WARNINGS

- Make sure your dog heeds a 'Quiet!' or 'Hush!' command. She can still guard the house, but can be quieted when the baby is asleep.
- Get a reign on jumping up before the baby comes home, and make sure her nails are trimmed.
- Never leave your dog alone with the baby. Even the best-behaved dog can become frustrated with a baby's cries and will act instinctively.

ONLINE RESOURCES

Dogs and Baby:

doggonesafe.com
tiny.cc/IntroduceDogBaby
tiny.cc/PetcoDogBaby

Cats and Baby:

tiny.cc/CatsBaby

Child Care Selection Guidelines

As more women continue with their careers after childbirth, and families are faced with the reality that two incomes are a necessity, childcare has become inevitable for many families. As a new father you may not be aware that you have some options when it comes to choosing child-care, and more importantly, you also have the responsibility of finding a safe and reliable provider.

Various Options

There are four basic options of child-care:

- **Formal child-care center:** Part of a chain or a non-profit. Typically large and take children from as young as 6 weeks up until school age. Required to be licensed and have state mandated staffing ratios.
- **Family day-care home:** Run directly out of a child-care provider's home. Will take much fewer children than a center, but may not require a license to be run. Usually less expensive than a center.
- **In-home care:** Live-in nanny or au pair is the most expensive option but provides care within arm's reach.
- **Family or friends:** Less structured arrangement (usually). May be cheapest option, however, especially if grandparents are the caregivers.

Tips for Selecting a Provider

There are a few basic things to keep in mind when evaluating any caregiver.

- **Verify accreditation/licensing:** Child Care Aware (**childcareaware.org**) is a great resource to check on specific state's licensing requirements. You can also use your state's licensing bureau to check past complaints about a specific provider. Remember that some states don't require home-based providers to be accredited, so be extra thorough when researching these types of providers and do background checks and contact more than one previous employer. Find more information at babysitters.com and NACCRRA.net.
- **Check references:** Also take the time to talk to parents picking up/dropping off kids outside the facility.
- **Tour the center:** Tours should be encouraged and staff should be open and attentive to any questions you have. Make at least one unscheduled visit in addition

> " After interviewing several people we finally chose [a live-in nanny]. But after two weeks I didn't feel right about this person. So, we got rid of her and went through the interviewing process again. The one we hired the second time around is still with us."
>
> — Veteran Dad

TRUST YOUR INSTINCTS

If you're unsure about a provider during the interview process, go with your intuition and steer clear. Even if you can't say what bothers you, it's better to trust your instincts and find someone you do trust.

to the initial scheduled tour. Any provider that isn't completely open with information or has a problem with your thoroughness should be absolutely avoided.

- **Check the space:** Ensuring that the facility is child-proof should go without saying, but your child's safety should always be a top priority so a comprehensive look over the child-care center is essential.

- **Observe the employees:** For toddlers, the child to caregiver ratio should never be more than 4-1 (under 12 months should be 3-1). Observe director and employee interaction and inquire about employee turnover rates; the lower the better. Verify employees are CPR certified, and ask to see current certifications.
- **Verify drop-in and pick-up policies:** Be wary about places that limit times when parents can stop by (one exception might be prescribed nap times, though). You should have access to your child whenever you want. Confirm the center will only release a child to a parent or authorized family member.

Final Thoughts

There is conflicting research about the effects of child-care. In a good environment, child-care can contribute to intellectual and social development, and yet children who spend more time in child-care have slightly more potential for behavior and learning issues. Since most of us don't have many options when it comes to childcare just do your best to find the right place for your child. Once placed, though, remember to keep your guard up. While most children respond well to a strong, nurturing care environment you still want to be on the lookout for extended behavioral and developmental inconsistencies that crop up after the child is in a care setting.

" We asked the grandparents to watch the Happiest Baby DVD so that they knew the system when he was crying."

— New Mom

FAMILY CARE

While often cost effective, family care can have its own drawbacks. Never hesitate to remove your child from an environment where your wishes as a parent aren't being kept (not laying your infant on her back for naps, for example). This can be difficult if it's grandma whose caring for the child, but your child's health and safety are more important than bruised egos.

CHILDCARE SELECTION GUIDE

tiny.cc/childcarequestions

Developed by a Veteran Mom from Boot Camp for New Moms, this extensive list of questions to ask potential childcare providers will give you an idea of what to consider when deciding who will watch your child.

Preparing for when He Is Sick

When to Call the Doctor

Whether it's coughing, diarrhea, crossed eyes, not eating, or anything else, if you think your baby is ill for any reason then check with a nurse hot line or your pediatrician. When it comes to your baby's health, err on the side of calling the doctor too often, as you may not be able to tell the big problems from little ones. Just call the doctor (that's what the doctors tell us). She will let you know if you are calling too much. It's also essential to get to know your baby's doctor by going to his well-baby checks. Go with mom or take turns with her.

Become the Family Paramedic

As Chief Roughhousing Officer and many adventures with your child ahead, you should consider adding the role of family paramedic to assure a competent response to your child's health issues. Basic resources and requirements include:

- **Emergency Phone Numbers** – Keep number readily available (next to the phone) for: doctor, nurse hot line, the local emergency room, regional poison center, trustworthy neighbor, etc.

- **Nurse Hot Line** – Experienced pediatric nurses are readily available 24 hours a day by phone and will spend all the time you need talking about any issue related to your baby's health. They will also tell you if you need to contact your doctor. Find out which hot line your doctor recommends, and call for even minor reasons to get to know them.

- **Medical Guide** – Purchase the latest edition of a comprehensive guide from a reputable source such as the *American Academy of Pediatrics Guide to Your Child's Symptoms*, the *American Medical Association Family Medical Guide*, or the *Mayo Clinic Family Health Book*.

THE DREADED NOSE BULB

A baby cannot blow his nose, so you will need to do it for him using a nose bulb (looks like a small turkey baster). He will hate having it stuck up his nose and will thrash around, making it a very difficult maneuver. Lie him face-up on the bed, wrap your arm around his head and place your hand on his chest to keep him from moving. With your other hand squeeze the air out of the bulb, quickly place it gently but snuggly in one nostril, and let the bulb expand. Repeat in other nostril. Being quick is the key.

- **First Aid Kit & Guide** – When you need a bandage, antiseptic, or cream for a minor burn, you need it readily available, so keep a well stocked kit handy. Keep a concise first aid guide in your kit and take it with you on hikes and outings.

- **A First Aid Class** – Ensures your family will have a dad who knows what he's doing in an emergency. Information on classes and handling emergencies can be found at RedCross.org.

How to Tell If He's Not Well

Babies give signals when they aren't feeling well. The most obvious are fever, runny nose, cough or rash. There are also less obvious signals: seems lethargic or very cranky, not interested in anything or anyone around him, has little or no appetite, spitting up more than usual, or stools are either very hard or runny. The intensity and duration of such symptoms are also factors that will help you, a nurse or a doctor determine how to treat them.

Fevers and Colds

Fever is how a baby responds to an infection. If his temperature is over 101 degrees, he has a fever. If he's less than two months old and his temperature is higher than 100 degrees, if a low grade fever has lasted longer than a few days, or if there is a rash along with the fever call your pediatrician.

Sniffles and respiratory congestion can make your baby miserable. Make sure her airway is clear and that she is not having difficulty breathing. Call the doctor if your baby's cough comes from deep in her chest, if her breathing is labored, or if she is wheezing.

Teething

Most babies get their first teeth between 4 and 6 months. As the teeth grow, they push through the baby's gums, which can be very painful. Drooling is the first sign of teething and there may be a slight fever. Most babies will let you know loudly that they are uncomfortable. Give him a teething ring that has been cooled in the refrigerator to chew on. Your knuckle will also work. Rubbing Oragel™(a topical pain reliever) on his gums

ONLINE RESOURCES

Keep these sites handy for more information what to do if your baby seems sick:

www.mayoclinic.com/health/healthy-baby/PRO0022

www.parents.com/baby/health/sick-baby/

www.marchofdimes.com/baby/sickbabycare_calldoctor.html

tiny.cc/coldorserious

kidshealth.org/parent/general/body/fever.html

IMMUNIZATIONS

immunizationInfo.org

Immunize.org

Immunofacts.com

> " If you don't have a first aid kit, you should get one."
> — Veteran Dad

Dealing with Her Symptoms

How to Prevent SIDS

While still a common fear, the incidence of SIDS has dropped in half due to the American Academy of Pediatric's Back to Sleep campaign, which recommends that you:

- Put your baby to sleep on her back with no toys, loose blankets, pillows, quilts, or other soft materials. This goes for nighttime, daytime naps, as well as naps at grandma's house.
- Do not allow smoking around your baby by anyone.
- Dress your baby in light sleep clothing so he does not overheat and keep the room at a comfortable temperature.
- Consider buying a sleep sack, especially in colder climates.

Most SIDS deaths occur at 2 to 4 months; after 6 months, the risks are minimal.

> " One of the things my wife was concerned about was SIDS and our friends told us about this pad that you can put under their bed or blanket and it senses their heartbeat. I don't know if it works, but if your wife worries like mine, it was worth it to make her happy."
>
> — Veteran Dad

Falls and Bumps on the Head

No matter how careful you are your baby will fall. If he tumbles off a couch, falls out of his high chair or slips out of your arms after a bath, you should do a thorough check for injuries and watch him closely for a while

CIRCULATING AIR REDUCES RISK

Dr. De-Kun Li, a Research Scientist at Kaiser Permanente in Northern California and a "proud father of two wonderful children," became interested in sudden infant death syndrome and came up with a brilliant notion: if SIDS is caused by a baby "rebreathing" still/stale air, a fan that circulates the air around him could help prevent SIDS. To test his hypothesis, Dr. Li and colleagues assessed information on 185 infants who died of SIDS and 312 other babies who did not die of SIDS.

His research, reported October 2008 in the Archives of Pediatrics and Adolescent Medicine, found that using a fan in a baby's room with poor ventilation apparently reduces the risk of SIDS by 72%.

Dr. Li cautions that additional research is needed to confirm the findings.

afterwards. If he cries after he falls, it's a good sign that he's not seriously injured. If he has fallen on his head or back, be even more careful in your observations. Watch him carefully for 24 hours. Take him to the doctor or emergency room if he:

- Seems weak or confused.
- Is having trouble moving any part of his body or there seems to be a deformity of an arm or leg.
- There is blood in the whites of his eyes or pink fluid coming out of his nose or ears.
- Shows signs of a concussion, such as crossed eyes or pupils that are unequal in size, or if he vomits.
- Cries loudly when you move any part of his body.
- Is sleeping more than normal.

Raising a Road Warrior

While you want to be careful in the first 6 weeks when their immune systems are just cranking up, there is no reason to keep a healthy baby at home. Make sure the diaper bag is fully stocked for an outing that will last more than several hours; if all day, add a daypack with extra diapers, undershirts, footed pajamas, an extra blanket, bottles and a few of his favorite toys. Include a plastic bag for disposing of diapers.

If the temperature is over 75°F, a diaper and t-shirt underneath a pair of footed pajamas is usually good enough. If it's breezy, add a light jacket and a hat to keep the sun off his face and his head warm. Add layers as the temperature gets lower.

> " I guess the most surprising thing was that none of the 200 terrible things I thought may happen did happen."
> — Veteran Dad

> **WARNING!**
>
> Don't give your baby any medicine without first checking with your pediatrician. A small dose of an adult pain reliever or decongestant may seem reasonable, but a baby's nervous and immune systems are very different from yours and present special issues that you are unlikely to be aware of.

> " That first night you're not going to sleep at all because everytime the baby moves, you're wondering if he's ok."
> — Veteran Dad

CHAPTER 7

Building A Family

> **"** Nobody ever says, 'Hey, Daddy, thanks for knocking out the rent. I sure love this hot water. It's easy to read with all this light...' "
>
> — Chris Rock

Preparing for Your Family's Future

From the moment you know your new baby is on the way, chances are you'll spend time worrying about how to make ends meet. This section will help you get a handle on the important issues you face:

Get a Handle on Your Finances

- **Get on the same page:** First, sit down with your partner and discuss the realities of your family's finances and what you are thinking about regarding new costs, income changes, lifestyle changes, etc.
- **Put a simple budget together:** Sort through your family's income and expenses. When you first run the numbers, if costs outweigh revenue, consider it normal.
- **Estimate increased expenses:** Such as diapers, day care, increase in health insurance premiums, any life/disability insurance you want to add.

Decide on One or Two Incomes

About half of new moms return to work within a few months after birth. You and/or your partner may want to quit your job and stay home with the baby. Perhaps it makes more sense for you to stay home. Perhaps she (or you) could work part time with the baby in day care a few days a week, or one of you could work from home. Think through some alternatives, and consider the costs of employment including taxes, day care, commuting, etc.

Seeing exactly by how much, and for how long, you expect your cumulative income to drop will indicate how much you need to cut back or have in savings to tide you over.

Major Changes May Be Appropriate

If you have a big mortgage that is dependent upon two incomes, you may want to reconsider being house rich even with a baby on the way. If you have a long commute that adds hours away from home on top of a long workday, you might want to look at

HEALTH INSURANCE TO-DOS

Contact your insurance provider and ask how much you'll need to pay out of pocket and if you face any restrictions on your choice of health-care facilities. Also, arrange to have your newborn added to your plan; this is usually required within 30 days and it's up to you to get it handled.

" I took on the role of protector when she got pregnant and I felt like a big part of that was making sure our family finances were in order, which started with making sure the hospital money was handled, all the way to starting a college fund."

– Veteran Dad

employment or housing alternatives. Moving or changing jobs is increasingly common during the ramp up to "D-day", and major lifestyle changes involving how and where you want to raise a family are increasingly common.

If She Doesn't Have Insurance

About 13% of women who become pregnant each year do not have health insurance. If your partner is not insured, it is important that you check out alternatives and resources early so that she receives appropriate prenatal care. The cost of delivery alone is $6,000 – $8,000 for a normal pregnancy and higher with a high risk pregnancy. Suggestions:

- Check out Medicaid, a federally funded program for low income persons. They will accept women who are already pregnant.
- Contact an obstetrician's or hospital's patient accounts department and ask about their policies and your alternatives. They can refer you to resources in your region, including Medicaid.
- Healthcare discount plans may be helpful (try americanpregnancy.org or ameriplan. org). First, ask your health care provider what discount you would receive if you paid cash. Ask about setting up a payment plan or if they offer a sliding scale.

> " I liked living near the beach, but we moved (inland) to reduce my commute as well as our mortgage payment so Mary doesn't have to go back to work for a while."
>
> — Veteran Dad

- If you are having an uncomplicated pregnancy, consider giving birth at a birthing center. Typically, the cost will be much lower. Many birth centers also provide sliding scales, payment plans and accept Medicaid. Despite planning on an uncomplicated pregnancy, you should check what their procedures are if an emergency does arise.
- Ask about insurance coverage for your baby as well. The State Children's Health Insurance Program (CHIP) is designed to help children in working families with incomes too high to qualify for Medicaid.

> " There's an entire industry designed to take advantage of your cluelessness as a new parent and make sure you purchase things out of guilt or stress. Just remember millions of kids are raised in mud huts next to wood fires."
>
> — Veteran Dad

Family Finance & Administration

When Money Is Tight

- Buy baby furniture second-hand, or borrow it from friends or family. There are a great number of stores that recycle baby items – lots of it is brand new – castoffs from baby showers or duplicate gifts. Just make sure they're compliant with today's standards for infant safety, and that they haven't been recalled.
- Mail out baby announcements to friends and relatives. Many will want to send gifts, gift certificates or money. Make sure you have registered at a baby store or big department store so people will be able to get you what you want and need.
- Register with online sites, such as babycenter.com and you'll not only get good information, you'll also get coupons and discounts on baby stuff.

Prepare for the Unthinkable

As new parents, you will have the very heavy responsibility of making arrangements in case something happens and you are not there to care for your child. While doing this ahead of time is prudent, mom will be very sensitive to the notion of leaving her baby without a mother, so use your discretion. Major tasks include:

- Make out a will (each parent needs one) or arrange a living trust. If you have access to legal assistance, take advantage. If not, economical on-line resources are available at legalzoom.com, nolo.com, legalconnection.com or findlaw.org.
- Specify who will care for your child if you are both unable to do so. This may take some time to work out if an obvious choice is not available. Write it down and make

sure that person knows they have been chosen and agrees to do it.
- Consider purchasing life insurance on the breadwinner(s) to assure basic financial support for your family. Term insurance, which pays off in the event of your death, is the least expensive. Check out efinancial.com or moneycentral.msn.com for the best rates.

Get an Early Start on His College Education

Typically the final gift you will want to give your child before you send him off into the world is financial support for college. It can be expensive, but "529" plans, administered in 48 states, help by providing investment opportunities to parents and grandparents with state and federal tax-deferred growth and tax-free withdrawals for qualified higher education expenses. Each state determines its plan's structure. There can also be a state tax deduction, a matching grant, scholarships, protection from creditors and exemption from state financial aid calculations. There are also plans that allow for the pre-purchase of tuition at colleges based on today's tuition rates. For more information, visit collegesavings.org.

Get Organized

With a baby on the way, it's a good idea to put together a well organized system for filing important documents. One way to do it is to create a hanging file for each broad category and fill it with manila folders for more specific topics. With the system in place, you'll have quick access to whatever you need, whenever you need it. Examples of typical family files:

- ❑ Birth Certificates
- ❑ Social Security Numbers
- ❑ Medical Records & Expenses
- ❑ House & Car Expenses
- ❑ Credit Cards
- ❑ Mortgage or Rental Contracts
- ❑ Insurance Papers
- ❑ Taxes
- ❑ Wills or Family Trust Documents

Make sure to carefully label every file. Better yet, buy a family/home organizing system that comes in a notebook or file box with pre-printed files for important contacts, wills, bank documents, etc.

❝ My wife and I just bought a new house and there's no way we can afford to keep it on one income. Yeah it was hard to leave Jessica with a babysitter, but we got over it."

– Veteran Dad

Recording Your New Family

Tips for Taking Pictures or Filming the Birth

- Check with your hospital on rules regarding photography or video.
- If you make the decision to appoint someone other than yourself to be the photographer, go with him or her to the hospital and ask to take a tour of the birthing area. It's also a good idea to watch a film of an actual birth in advance.
- Make a decision, along with your partner, about how intimate you want the filming to be. Consider black and white photos if you decide to capture the moment without the graphic elements.
- Capture the details; facial expressions, dad and mom working together, mom as she rests between contractions, holding the baby for the first time, etc.
- Avoid using a flash or bright light. It can distract and annoy mom (and the hospital staff). Don't use a flash to shoot the baby as he's being born – it might hurt his eyes.
- The photographer needs to understand that there are more important priorities during labor and birth.
- When the baby arrives, capture her face. Ask the attending nurse where to stand for the best view.
- Make sure you have a picture of yourself with your baby for the first time.

More Photos as She Grows

- **Document Her Development:** Take a series of pictures once a week/month that represent your baby's growth and developmental stages. By using the same location each time, the pictures will evolve into a story without words.
- **Unplanned (Candid) Shots are Best:** Just try to get him doing his thing.
- **Use Natural, Soft Light:** With natural light, your baby's face will glow; camera flashes and indoor lamps can make your baby's skin appear mottled. Using natural light is best, and most cameras will tell you when you don't have enough light to take a good shot. Try opening the drapes or window shades or moving to an area with more sun light.
- **Take Lots of Pictures from Different Angles:** Shoot your baby from above as she's looking up at you. Most people never think of taking photos of the backs of their babies, but these can be great shots and an interesting way to capture body language.
- **Baby's-Eye View:** Don't be afraid to get down and dirty when taking baby pictures. Photos taken on their level are charming, to say the least.
- **Try Black and White:** Black and white pictures accentuate the details of your baby's face and body, plus it gives them a nostalgic and classic feel.

Sharing and Organizing

Online photo-sharing websites such as Shutterfly, Flickr, Picasa etc., are a great way to share photos of your little one with friends and family. You and they can order books, calendars, etc. with baby as the star.

These sites will store your photos, but you might consider getting an external hard drive to keep the originals in a safe place. It's extra work on the front-end, but creating well-labled albums/folders and tagging/categorizing photos as you upload them now will assure you'll easily be able to find photos years from now. (At least date the folder and give a couple-word description.)

If you're going to post photos on Facebook or other public sites, think about whether you want to use your child's real name, nickname, initial, etc.

Getting Good Video

Be selective about what you are shooting. Think about what you plan to shoot and how you can best capture it before flipping on the "record" switch. After you get what you want, pause the tape and wait for your next opportunity.

Avoid jerky movements and pause the recording when going from one person to another. Try not to stay on one thing for too long, and focus on details.

Keep your camera in a safe, but easily accessible place, she probably won't wait for you to get the camera out of the back of the closet before taking her first steps.

Announce It

Before the baby's born, go ahead and pick out the announcements you want to send.

If you're going to send announcements through the mail, print up a sheet of address labels and make sure you have enough stamps. (If you have the envelopes already, get them ready.) If you're sending online, get all the email addresses together.

There are dozens of websites that send e-announcements and traditional hard copies. Take advantage of free photo offers from photo-sharing sites to make your own (mostly) free announcements or to send photos with your announcements.

DON'T FORGET TO BACK-UP

You will probably find yourself using your cell phone for pictures and video on-the-go.

While easy and attached to your hip, all those memories are a drop, water incident or missplaced phone away from being gone forever.

Learn how to manually back up your phone to your computer and/or check with your carrier or phone manufacturer to see if they offer a free back up app/service.

Your iPhone might be able to back up to ICloud and if you use the Google+ app, you can turn on the "Instant Upload" feature to back up photos and video.

> " I was taking so many pictures that if I didn't keep them organized, they turned into a big mess."
> — Veteran Dad

Creating Traditions & Memories

Want Do You Want Your Children and You to Remember Doing?

The best memories often come from the traditions and rituals that you develop as a family. Parents can strengthen the family by creating memories through activities like planning camping trips with dad and making a tradition out of how you celebrate birthdays and holidays, bedtime routines, religious activities, and dinner time. Merely repeating an activity every year makes it special and makes it a part of family lore.

Your children will come to expect the event which will help guarantee it keeps happening and over time becomes a shared memory. These fond memories give your child a sense of security, stability, and belonging along with pride in his family.

> " There were 5 kids in our family and my dad was a doctor and worked long hours. But every Saturday he would spend with us kids and we would all go do something. We would do things like go to Disneyland, out to lunch, hiking, anything we wanted to do. We knew we could always count on it and we all loved it. I think my mom was the one that loved it the most, though."
>
> — Veteran Dad

INDIAN STORIES

If there ever was anything I ever did right as a dad, it was telling my children stories.

I had never told one in my life before, but when I had a one and four year old, I found inspiration in a long ago Native American ancestor. Our stories evolved around an Indian family that just happened to be like ours (they added two more children as well), and those kids did cool and amazing things. Like caring for a baby eagle and returning him to his nest, taming horses and inventing irrigation. We were even involved with warring tribes, but always were the peace makers.

Of course dad was a cool and amazing Chief, brave and strong with a great bod and a tribe that happily followed his lead. (Hey, they were my stories).

Never Too Soon

Starting a tradition with a baby may seem a little premature, but since the tradition's longevity makes it stronger, it's never too early to start.

- Create your own rituals from scratch. Some you'll borrow from your past but you can also get creative.
- Although your baby seems unaware right now, he's absorbing every sight and sound around him. For instance, he will be captivated by the bright colors, sparkling lights, and music of the holiday season or Fourth of July.
- Watch past holiday celebrations on video.
- Give your special tradition a catchy name making it fun and memorable. Sunday mornings while mom sleeps in can become the "fun day club" with dad.
- A tradition of spontaneity: Create some amazing memories on a whim. Instead of heading home after the game, hit the road and take an overnight trip to an amusement park or historical monument.
- Create personal traditions between dad and child.
- Repeat the personal tradition with each child as they reach a particular age or milestone. For example, when each child reaches age 14 take them on a special trip.

" My previously busy working life schedule was not really all that important. Time with my daughter was."

— Veteran Dad

Memorable Ideas

- Sing your favorite songs together.
- Read stories or books aloud together.
- Snuggle together in mom and dad's bed on Saturday mornings.
- Give out nicknames (the little things count).
- Make breakfast with the kids on Saturdays.
- Pitch a tent and rough it with the kids.
- Share interests such as gardening, woodworking, singing, baking, hiking, or playing an instrument.
- Play board games one night a week.
- Share the value of being generous.
- Attend church services on Sunday.
- Drive out to the country to pick a pumpkin.
- Take an annual trip to cut down the Christmas tree.
- Hang stockings by the chimney with care.
- Have a one-on-one every night before your child goes to bed (especially if you take frequent business trips).
- Make bath time an event with a special song or game.
- Participate in bedtime rituals such as telling or reading a story, singing a song, or saying a prayer.
- Get the extended family together for Sunday dinner on a weekly—or monthly—basis with grandparents, aunts, uncles, and cousins.
- Discover the traditions of your ancestors by exploring your racial or cultural history.
- Tell family stories (true stories and legends).
- Prepare traditional foods that honor your heritage.
- Take a family photo in the same spot every year.

Learning More and Getting Help

Whatever problems you may experience as a new father, always remember you are not alone, and as a result, there are resources available to you and your new family. To help you learn more about your circumstances, and if necessary, to get help, we have compiled the online New Father Resource Center on DadsAdventure.com. Check it out for updates and additions, or to recommend new resources that may help other fathers. Below is a representation of organizations and web sites from the online resource center that address issues encountered by dads and offer information to help you and your partner.

CHILD ABUSE

National Child Abuse Hotline
ChildHelpUSA.org
1-800-4-A-CHILD
For parents seeking help with feelings of frustration and violence.

National Institute for Neurological Disorders and Stroke Shaken Baby Information Page
tiny.cc/NINDS_ShakenBaby
Links to resources and information on abusive behavior, signs of infant abuse.

ThinkFirst.org
tiny.cc/ThinkFirstShakenBaby
Fast facts on shaken baby syndrome

CIGARETTE CESSATION

Smoke Free
smokefree.gov
Tools and online and telephone help for quitting smoking.

American Cancer Society
tiny.cc/ACS_QuitSmoking
Guide to Quitting Smoking

WebMD
www.webmd.com/smoking-cessation
Resources, blogs, articles, community

CONFLICT AND ANGER MANAGEMENT

Relationship911.org
Information about conflict in a variety of different relationship
scenarios. A resource for articles and books, as well as online help.

ConflictCenter.org
Workshops in their Denver location, or sign up to receive the online newsletter.

DRUG AND ALCOHOL ASSISTANCE

Alcoholics Anonymous
aa.org
Resources to help with addiction.

National Organization on Fetal Alcohol Syndrome
www.nofas.org/family
Information on drinking and pregnancy.

Drug Abuse Treatment
drug-abuse-treatment.us
Information on different types of treatment for drug abuse and where to find help near you.

GRIEF/LOSS

Grief Recovery Online for All Bereaved (GROWW)
www.groww.org/resource.htm
Many great links to organizations and online resources to help deal with the loss of an infant and recovering from grief in general.

Center for Loss in Multiple Birth, Inc.
climb-support.org
Organization that provides parent-to-parent support for those who have experienced the death of one or more multiple birth children.

IVF.com/misc.html
Article with information dealing with the loss of a baby.

PREEMIES

March of Dimes
www.modimes.org
Articles and state by state contacts information

Resources for Parents of Preemies
tiny.cc/preemies
Articles, one-to-one support, dads club.

> " As the dad, you need to be able to find the resources for your family."
>
> — Veteran Dad

Babies with Special Needs

There are many books and resources that address the issues surrounding babies with special needs. Our purpose here is to touch on a few of the key points that have specific implications for fathers.

There are over 300 categories of birth defects and developmental disabilities listed in the National Birth Defect Registry. Most types are rare; for example, hypoplastic left heart syndrome affects about 3 of every 10,000 babies, and cleft lip with or without cleft palate affects about 1 of every 1,000 babies.

From autism to scoliosis, however, one in 33 babies in the U.S. is born with some sort of birth defect. While it is inconceivable to most people that their baby might have a disorder, it does happen.

Sometimes parents find out about a disability, such as Down syndrome, during pregnancy. At other times, there's a dramatic surprise, a cleft palate or heart problem, which surfaces at birth or later on.

It goes without saying that babies born with disabilities will require extra care. However, the extra care required is not usually as demanding as the psychological process we must confront as parents of a baby with special needs.

Receiving the News

Whether during the pregnancy or after the birth, the news of a birth defect shatters our fantasy of what it will be like to be a dad and leaves us facing a vast unknown. Dads who have confronted this challenge agree - your baby needs you now more than ever. Your baby must have everyone in her corner, advocating for her and seeking to understand how best to care for her.

ONLINE RESOURCES

specialchildren.about.com
tiny.cc/SpecialNeedsBaby
Information and resources on special needs babies
childrenwithspecialneeds.com
For Parents, By Parents

> " I learned that even when a baby isn't capable of interaction, the baby still needs the dad's hold and touch to balance the woman's hold and touch. There's something that brings a calmness to the baby. When it's just all mommy, the baby tends to fuss a lot more."
> – Veteran Dad

Be prepared for the fact that, especially at first, even your closest friends and relatives may not know how to help you deal with your new situation. They may ask hurtful questions, offer bad advice, or generally just shy away until they figure out how to handle their own emotional responses.

It is critical that you and mom stick together. Talk to her early and often so you both know what is going on with each other. Anticipate that bonding and loving your child will be harder, which in turn can lead to serious guilt.

Give It Time

It is likely that your vision of fatherhood includes an image of you and a child that runs, plays, and laughs. You may see yourself in the future passing on your wisdom to this child that represents the continuing generations of your family. If your child has a disability, this vision may require realignment.

Coming to grips with your child's new realities does not happen quickly. The initial shock of finding out usually gives way to a long period of denial. Somewhere within these two stages the flight-or-fight response is triggered, sending some dads running from their family, trying to escape this daunting challenge.

Running, of course, is not an option for you. In fact, by hanging in there and giving it time, you will be building a bond with your child that is deeper than anything you imagined prior to his birth.

Circle the Wagons

The most effective way to focus your worries and concerns on something productive is to start assembling your resource team. This will include friends, family, medical experts, and some form of emotional counsel. The best place to begin is the hospital where your baby was born. Often the staff that is treating your baby will be your first resource for basic medical advice about your baby's particular condition and how to care for your baby properly. The hospital's social worker will know of resources in your community that can be helpful in supporting you.

THE LOSS OF A BABY

The only outcome more unthinkable than a child born with a disability is one that is still-born or dies shortly after birth. Although you don't want to dwell on this possibility, it is important to remember that most hospitals have loss and grief support for parents dealing with this circumstance. The process usually includes on-going individual counseling for both parents as well as groups for parents who have lost a baby.

This form of support typically has two goals. One goal is to help the family work through the myriad emotions associated with the death of a baby and the other is to help the family incrementally evaluate their readiness to have another child. For some couples this is a relatively quick process and for others it can take a while. In the end most couples who have lost a child at or shortly after birth go on to have another pregnancy that results in a successful outcome.

Making a Family with a Special Baby

Avoid the Blame Game

As with any situation that feels out of our control, a baby born with a disability or illness can trigger in us a need to blame something or someone. Often mothers take on the guilt for not having produced a perfect child, even if the cause of the disability runs in the genetics of the father's side of the family. The point here is that no matter what, blaming another for the situation you are in will only delay the necessary process of getting to know and love your child and at the same time could cause a fracture in your marriage.

Make Your Relationship Stronger

You might hear that a child who is ill or disabled will make you and your partner feel closer, but this is not necessarily true – especially at first. The added demands impact every area of your life. Work, friends, family relationships, finances, and self-concept are just a few of the areas that take a hit. So the question becomes: what can you do to help your relationship weather the storm? The answer is, a lot.

- **Don't isolate.** A baby who is different makes for parents who are different from other parents. It is easy to feel cut off from the support that you need as a couple if you can't share common challenges with parents who understand where you're coming from. Search your community for parent groups that are geared to parents of children with special needs.
- **Seek professional help.** One of the keys to pulling together with your partner is sharing your perspective with someone who is experienced with the situation you are going through. This kind of support can create a safe environment to explore the issues and emotions associated with caring for your baby as well as your relationship.

- **Validate your partner.** Every mother needs to know she is a good mom. This concept is tantamount as it applies to the mother of a child with special needs. You can strengthen your connection with your partner by giving her positive feedback about her skill as a mom. Spend time on a regular basis pointing out all your child can do, see, and hear instead of only what they can't.
- **Practice self-care.** You will be the most help to your family if you take care of yourself. Take a bit of time each day to do something you enjoy. Even 30 minutes will strengthen your ability to cope with stress and help you keep a positive perspective.

A Deeper Kind of Love

If you hang in there and stay focused on what is important, the chaos surrounding your unexpected circumstances will give way to loving your child for who they are. Parents who successfully navigate these turbulent waters find that they come to a place where they are able to celebrate their child's smallest victories and accomplishments. This is where you're headed and when you get there you will know it because your heart will be filled with pride, humility, and love. Start by spending as much hands-on time as possible with your baby and learn how to care for him.

> " When we first found out he had down syndrome, it was such a crazy time we didn't know if we would make it through. And we didn't know if our marriage would make it. But, two years in to it, we wouldn't change a thing about him."
>
> — Veteran Dad

CHAPTER 8

Making It An Adventure

"Take your baby out on your own. It gives mom a break...and it gives her confidence that you can bring the baby back alive."
— Veteran Dad

Make Your Fatherhood an Adventure

Get Ahead of the Curve

Babies are a lot of work and caring for them can be very boring, especially if you decide to wait until they learn to play catch to have fun. Get ahead of the curve by turning mundane tasks with your child into mini-adventures, and building up to bigger ones as they grow. This will get you both ramped up for the magical years of ages roughly 3-10 (longer for girls) when they think that you are the greatest person on earth. Do this and they might stick with you through their teen years (dream on).

With a couple of decades ahead of you two, the sky is the limit when it comes to having fun and adventures together. So now is the time to start planning and doing.
- Check out the 0-3 Months Adventure list on *page 132*.
- At 6 months, the child you want to teach to surf can start swimming lessons.
- A 2 year old is a great assistant for gardening, and they are amazed at how tall and fast corn grows.

Dad's adventure isn't necessarily an Indiana Jones style excursion through an abandoned tomb with your toddler strapped to your back. Although with appropriate safety measures, it could be.

Take a Hike

Get a good baby backpack carrier that goes easy on your back, and start with short trips to lengthen his attention span and get yourself in shape. That way when your hike together turns magical, with him jabbering away about the cool rocks you hand him, you and he will be comfortable and want to keep going. You won't need a diaper bag for short hikes, but a jacket for weather changes, sunscreen, a hat and a small First-Aid kit will keep you well prepared.

> " When guys are connected to their children early, there's more likelihood that they'll stay connected."
>
> – Veteran Dad

Re-live Your Own Childhood Adventures & Plan on New Ones

What were the things you liked best about your own childhood? They make great traditions with your own child, so start early and invite your own dad to join in. Camping and fishing are classics, and you can start her off in the backyard and bathtub.

Organize Outings with Other Dads

New dads stuck at home with a baby will jump at an invitation to join you and your baby on a Saturday morning at a coffee house and then an outing. A father in Marin, California started a group that goes hiking with their babies in backpacks (A.K.A. "Grateful Dads"), and so can you. Nothing like getting together with friends, co-workers, guys from childbirth classes, etc., to trade stories, learn new techniques, blow off steam, and create a "nursery in a locker room" setting.

Girls Can Do Anything Boys Can Do

Picturing our sons playing in the NFL comes naturally, but girls, well, they do girl things and then fall in love with some guy with questionable motives. Our instincts tell us to rough-house with our sons, but to hug and protect our daughters. So you can see it's easy to shortchange our baby girls right from the start (same with our boys when it comes to hugs). So start her early. She definitely benefits from rough-housing with you; research shows that girls whose fathers engage them in sports grow up to enjoy better fitness, stronger self images, and healthier, lasting relationships later on in life with men (on that note, teach her a martial art).

'...DO WHAT YOU ALWAYS WANTED'

"You may think a baby means you will no longer be able to do the things you like to do. Actually, a child can provide the opportunity to do what you always wanted to do."

My first OB said this to us guys and it turned out to be true. Learning to ride horses with my daughter, play paint ball with my sons, being another daughter's pitching coach, taking all my kids to explore some part of the world when they turned 14; all in addition to camping, fishing and starting backpacking at three.

- Greg Bishop, Author

" Once a month we get up early Saturday morning and head to the local car show. He loves seeing all the people and I love hanging out with guys that I'd gotten to know pre-baby. And it fells pretty good to carry him around on my chest."

— Veteran Dad

Other Dads Show You How

If you think about the adventures you want to have together, whether it's teaching him to fish, surf, work on cars or name the stars, you are not only more likely to do these things, you realize how much you have to look forward to with your child. To help you get going, we offer examples of other dads' adventures with their kids:

Racing

It may not seem an obvious choice to invite your daughter to ride along while you compete in a Baja ProTruck race at Pikes Peak, but Rob Reinertson had his 17-year-old daughter Christine as his co-driver for the 15-minute competition. After relaying information about upcoming twists and turns to her father while being jostled around in his race truck, Christine said the experience was one of the highlights of her life.

Surfing

Paul Solotaroff's son Luke is afflicted with a rare genetic syndrome similar to autism. After years of struggling to find an activity to stimulate Luke, Paul came across the idea of rehabilitative surfing. Just minutes into his first wave, Luke was exhibiting joy rarely seen by his parents. Now both father and son are learning to surf, spending time together, and Luke is experiencing significant improvement in motor skills, social skills, and behavior.

Cooking

Wayne Brachman – professional chef and author of several books on cooking – spends many nights a week shopping for groceries and cooking with his two daughters. Wayne's goal is to get his daughters thinking about food: expanding their palates; knowing where their food comes from; what it takes to prepare; and how it affects them. At the ages of 8 and 5 his daughters are already doing a significant portion of the cooking (under supervision), and have already developed a greater sense of the wider world of food (that is, beyond PB&J and Mac & Cheese).

LAUNCHING INTO SPACE

New York father Luke Geiss-buhler and his 7-year-old son Max used a weather baloon and some cleverness to launch an iphone and a video camera 20 miles off into space. After working on it for months, their capsule burst after reaching the upper atpmosphere, then came pachuting back to earth. They were able to recover the video of the flight and are already planning their next experiment.

> I put a small surfboard on the wall next to the crib and bath time is for learning to paddle. She mostly just splashes, but she's only 3-months old."
>
> — Veteran Dad

Building Boats

Paul Rollins has been rebuilding boats for 30 years, but now he's doing it with his son (22 at the time of the article) Paul Jr. Working out of two boat barns (one of which, Paul Jr. lives in) just feet from Paul Sr.'s house, the two spend their days restoring and building boats and it's Paul Sr.'s wish for Paul Jr. to one day take over the family business.

Skiing

On the urging of her father John, 5-year-old Anne Rostenberg would walk up a small hill near her home in an effort to get used to her skis. Thirty-five years later dad and daughter are still skiing together. Both say that it's their yearly ski trips that have helped to keep them so connected. Taking a cue from the Rosterbergs, Sean McCarthy is already skiing with his 3-year-old Julia, although she gets a tether and harness that's controlled by dad.

Karting

Enrolling his son in a short go-kart course to see "where he fell with it," Mike Distler could not have predicted that his son Woody would begin putting up race times one might expect of an older teen or adult who was familiar with racing. At age 11, labeling Woody a "prodigy" isn't a stretch of the imagination. Indy car racers Michael and Marco Andretti, and Sam Hornish Jr. are former kart racers who have made good on their early success.

Computers

David Moses and his 5-year-old daughter Zoe have been playing on computers together since she was 2. They work together on both hardware and software. Zoe has her own computer and is so comfortable with the ins and outs of computing, that she trains the other children in her class.

Survival Training

Sometimes there is an unexpected bonus from teaching your child about the outdoors. When 5-year-old Hannah Klamecki was swept away in a river from the island she and her grandfather were swimming to she made some important decisions that helped her survive. Her grandfather drowned after he was swept away, but Hannah, who had floaties on, had been exposed to the outdoors by her father. She drank water from the river and ate berries to survive the two days in the woods.

" Whether I'm building a wood desk for my home office or planting tomatoes in the backyard, I always include my two young kids in the task. They'll help me hammer a nail or mix the soil. They get a kick out of helping me and it also instills in them a love of work, which I learned from my own parents. The bonus – and a tip to the husbands out there – is that my wife is thrilled that things get done, and loves to show her appreciation for it!"

— Benjamin Bratt, actor, father of two

Adventures for 0 to 3 Months

1 Her Favorite Mug: For the first few weeks a baby's vision is fuzzy. She'll fixate on things that are about a foot from her eyes - like your face when you hold her. Let her check out your mug and grab your nose. Place a picture or toy with contrasting colors in his line of sight to catch his attention; then move it back and forth slowly so he can track it.

2 Monkey See, Monkey Do: Get close to her face and smile. Around four to six weeks she will start smiling back. Many babies will imitate your facial gestures, so open your mouth, widen your eyes, and of course, stick out your tongue. Even if she doesn't, keep trying, because this game can hold her attention for a long time.

3 Airplane: Hold your baby with both hands—one under her bottom and the other cupped on the back of her head and neck. Hold her up in the air and let her fly around slowly and gently. Always firmly support her head and keep it higher than her bottom.

4 Pull-ups: Put him on your lap facing up, place one finger in his hand so he grabs on, and pull it up a little. Then put another finger in his other hand so he grabs on with both hands. Pull him up just a little (keep his unsupported head on your lap), and then let him down and repeat.

5 Baby Calisthenics: Games involving limb movement are possible at this age, but you'll have to do most of the work. With your baby on her back, gently pull her legs up toward you and then side to side, talking to her the whole time. Do the same with her arms.

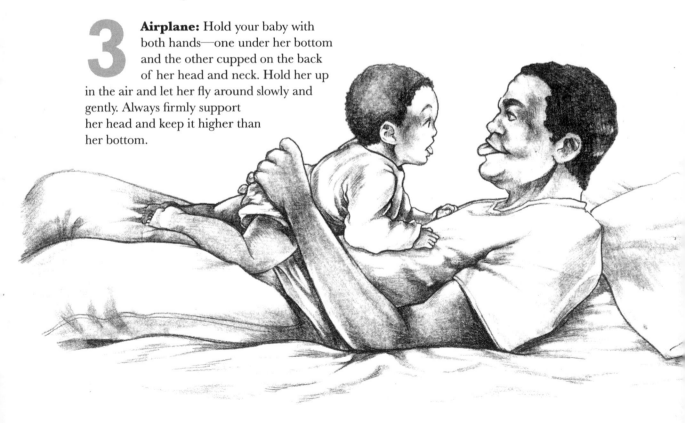

6 **Jumping Jacks:** With your baby on her back, raise her arms over her head and then put them down. Then take one arm and gently cross it over toward the opposite shoulder. Repeat with the other arm. While you're doing it, count off the moves (a one and a two and a three and a four).

7 **Walking at a Month:** Their walking reflex is very cool. Supporting him with both hands, stand him on the bed and lean him forward. He will slowly raise one foot as if to take a step, and if you move him forward, he will take another. Another amazing feat to show the guys.

8 **Belly Time:** Now that we put our babies to sleep on their backs to help prevent SIDS, they have less opportunity to develop their upper body strength by lifting their heads and pushing themselves up with their hands. So give him plenty of belly time while playing and he will be the first and fastest crawler in his Mommy & Me group.

9 **Kiss Her Hand:** Give her a chance to touch you in return. Letting her know how wonderful she is, and how all her moves are amazing will tell her you delight in her attempts, and she'll do it more and more. Tone it down when she turns 5; you don't want to embarrass her.

10 **Sit on Your Chest:** Lie down on your back with your baby sitting on your chest facing you. Let him explore your face. Enjoy his intense concentration as he checks everything out. Be careful because he may grab your nose and try to remove it.

11 **Elvis!:** Bruce Springsteen, Radiohead, The Killers or whatever you like. Once he starts rocking out, you can take him on tour to grandma's house. Got a comedy act buried deep? Time to drag it out. No matter how bad you are, he'll think you're the best.

> " When she wakes up in the morning, she gets all excited when she sees or hears me. You can't buy that type of feeling."
>
> — Veteran Dad

Best Tips from Boot Camp for New Dads

1 **Trust your instincts.** A little experience will quickly turn you into one of the world's leading experts on your own baby.

2 **Learn from the best.** Ask the hospital nursery personnel to show you how to change, swaddle and bathe your baby.

3 **When it comes to mom, be patient and positive.** Communication and support are the key. She'll love you for it.

4 **Stand your ground.** Let no one push you away from your baby. Not your mother-in-law, your mate, your boss, no one.

5 **Learn as a family, just the three of you.** Keep "help" in the first weeks down to what is needed lest it become interference.

6 **Your baby is portable.** You can take your baby anywhere. Don't get caught up in fretting about what you can't do.

7 **You will get frustrated.** Step back. Think. Count to some high number. Think again, and so forth.

8 **Make eye contact.** Babies talk with their eyes. You will see!

9 **Relax and enjoy the ride.** Make it a daily habit to play with your baby, check out her tiny little feet, have him fall asleep on your chest, etc. It's the little things that count.

10 **When times are trying, remember they will pass.** Before you know it, you will have a teenager on your hands.

11 **Set the tone you are here to play and change his first diaper** – ask the nurse to walk you through it.

12 **Becoming a father has highs and lows.** Getting informed and ready for whatever might happen is the best thing you can do. The lows can be tough, but the highs make it all more than worthwhile.

13 **Spend time alone with your baby away from mom.** This time on your own is when you build your strongest connection with your child.

14 **There is no one right way to be a dad.** Every baby, mom and dad is unique. You – along with mom – are the one to decide what works best for your new family.

15 **We learn best from fathers who are doing the job.** Talk to your brothers, friends and other dads around you. You can get stuff off your chest, gain some perspective or even get inspired.

16 **Most of what you need to know comes naturally.** Change his diapers, rock him to sleep, give him a bath, and in a week or two you'll feel like a natural.

17 **Fatherhood is about sacrifice, honor, and fulfillment as a man.** It takes time to adjust, so cut yourself some slack but never stop trying.

18 **Before she arrives, you won't know how important you'll be to your child**, or how important she'll be to you.

19 **No matter what happened during pregnancy**, remember **the rubber hits the road when the baby is born.** What happens after that is what counts.

20 In these over commercialized, hyper-compulsive child-rearing times - **don't sweat the small stuff.**

Advice from Experienced Fathers

1 You bring your own unique strengths to the job of parenting, and you should be confident that you are fully capable of caring for your baby. Develop your understanding and capabilities as a father, and focus on making the most of the practicality, creativity and stamina you bring to this task.

2 You'll be inspired to be a better father when you see great dads in action. Look to family members, friends, co-workers and other new dads you've met. If you connect and share experiences with other fathers, you will be surrounded by men who will help you do your best.

3 Loving your child at first sight, or at any time, is not automatic. Get involved, give it time, and keep up. Babies can be a wonderful source of joy and fulfillment, but they can also be boring, frustrating and irritating. How it all adds up is up to you. Prepare for the worst and take advantage of the best. The key is developing confidence before she arrives, and jumping in with both hands once she does.

4 While fatherhood is forever, it occurs one day at a time, and some days will be better than others. You are going to make mistakes, and each new day presents an opportunity to take another shot. It is a tough transition, and you must be patient with your baby, your mate, and yourself.

5 Fatherhood is about growing up and accepting responsibility. For most men, this takes time, so cut yourself some slack, but keep moving forward. We all have an instinctual desire in our heart to do right by our child, but stuff gets in the way. Those who do the job understand the rewards are well worth the sacrifices; those who skip out don't know what they are missing.

6 Next to confidence, a sense of humor is what will get you through the tough times. Laughing beats crying, so help yourself and mom see the lighter side.

7 The basic challenge you face is not changing diapers or comforting a crying baby, but forming a new family. The pressures and demands that babies bring often place a serious drag on your relationship. It is essential that you form a team approach that benefits the baby, strengthens your relationship and provides long term stability for your family.

8 The changes experienced by new moms can be tough and confusing, and moms in turn can be very tough on new dads. Part of the basic job description for new fathers is to serve as mom's virtual punching bag (you're not alone). We are built tough, and if we understand what's happening, we can take it.

9 Parenthood often comes at a time when work and other commitments are taking up most of your time. We tell ourselves we can "get to it later," but if you wait \to get involved with your baby, she'll be a toddler and you'll have missed out on her baby years. Spend time with her now.

10 If you don't take care of yourself, you won't be able to take care of your new family. Your health and well being is essential to all of you.

11 Develop unique things between you and your child that make you both feel important. Start with a funny face that lets him know it is playtime, progress to high fives, and as he grows, proceed to more complex maneuvers. It reminds you both that you are special to each other, an inseparable team.

Final Words of Wisdom

Your Baby Will Provide You a New Source of Strength

Given the opportunity, your baby will grab hold of your heart, motivate you to do your best, and add dimensions to your life that for now are unimaginable. Trust it will happen, look for opportunities to make it happen and then take full advantage when it does. As one smoking father trying to quit said, "every time I wanted a cigarette, I picked her up and looked in her eyes, and it was like she was asking me to do it for her."

Turn Your Buddies into Uncles

You need your buddies for balance in your life. Most men don't make friends easily, and after a baby arrives we tend to lose touch with those we do have. After being tied up at home before and after the birth, your friends get the idea that you are out of circulation. Jump back in by showing up with junior. After a few times asking, "can you hold her for a minute," they'll be reaching for her all the time. Show them how to feed her with the bottle, rock her to sleep, and of course how to do the tricks you have taught her. They will call to ask if you can bring her over to play.

> " There was a moment after all the birth stuff when my wife was exhausted and had fallen asleep and I was holding the baby. And I was looking at the baby and this magic happened. And all of a sudden, I said to myself, 'I'm a dad. I'm never going to be what I was before. I'm a new person.' "
>
> — Veteran Dad

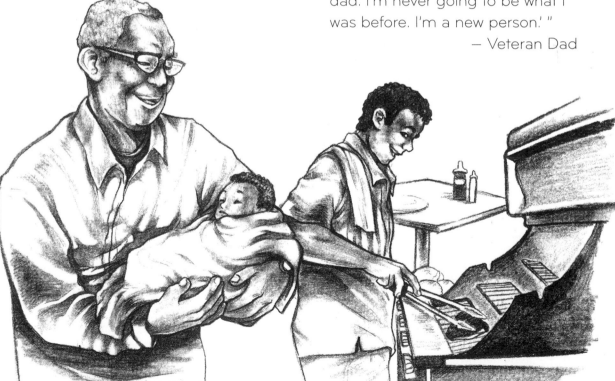

Make Your Fatherhood Your Own By Bringing Your Baby into Your World

New fatherhood has been described as a roller coaster ride in which just hanging on is a challenge. Once things settle down, start charting your own course as a dad rather than just getting swept along by the demands you face or even the course set by your wife. Make it your own by introducing your child to the things you enjoy, like sports, the outdoors or car shows (with her in a backpack), painting or music (they are naturals), or develop some new interests you can share.

Take Pride in What You Do

Becoming a father is the ultimate rite of manhood for those who step up to the challenge. You won't find a more rigorous trial, and whether you succeed or fail is entirely up to you. As men, at some point in our lives, we want to know what we are made of, and as a father, we get our chance to find out. Periodically assess how far you have come as a dad and the commitment you have made to your child. Accept any mistakes as the price of trying, and take pride in all that you do.

Engage Your Spirituality

We dads should gather all the strength we can muster to meet the challenges along our path, but one source many of us overlook is our spiritual dimension. Whether we report to a God through a formal religion, simply believe in God or even Karma, a new baby personifies the most wonderful of creations and the very meaning of life. Consider calling on all available spiritual powers to help you do your best as her dad.

> " In a sense, it's caused me to re-look at the way I see the world. Because James sees everything for the first time, and as we get older, we get somewhat jaded, tired, and kinda feel like we're being kicked around a bit. But to see through his eyes, you really see some of the great things about the world that you've forgotten about. It's almost being born for the second time."
>
> — Veteran Dad

You Will Get to Where You Want to Be as a Dad

Like new moms, we also struggle to adjust to our new responsibilities and go through a process of self-discovery. While we fathers have a longer transition to parenthood, ultimately we become different people as well. Tougher, better, more fulfilled men. As long as you keep trying, especially after tough periods that can take the wind out of your sails, you will get to where you want to be as a dad.

Introduce Him to Your Father

Grandfathers are often last in line, so make it special when it is time to introduce your baby to your own father. Take your baby and ask your dad to follow you alone into another room, show him how your baby likes to be held, and ask your dad – father to father – what he remembers about his newborns. Try it with your father-in-law too.

We Are All in This Together

One of the great things about Boot Camp workshops is that we get men from all walks of life. You'll see a young truck driver orient a corporate lawyer on the fine points of burping a baby, or an African-American veteran showing an Asian rookie how to change a diaper. And when those babies start crying, we all react the same way. At Boot Camp, men of different cultures, ages and incomes quickly find mutual respect when working together to learn how to care for their children. We found the same when we conducted a training program to set up Boot Camp for New Dads (AKA "Hit The Ground Crawling") in England with a group of teen fathers in Liverpool (check out a clip on DadsAdventure.com). It is clear that we fathers are all in this together.

> " One thing I've come to realize is that raising your children is a way to make a positive contribution to the world."
> — Veteran Dad

We Are Brothers

I have six brothers, and I can tell you that it feels very good to have other men respect and understand you and give you a hand when you need it. Over the past twenty-one years, Boot Camp has worked the same way: we respect and look out for each other, extend a hand through our advice and sometimes just listen. We are all brothers in a sense.

Let's Reach Out to Each Other

When you see another new dad, ask him how old his baby is and whether he is getting any sleep. Then with a nod to his baby, tell him "nice job." He will light up; you will have made his day. A quick glance of understanding to the father struggling with a crying child, will strengthen his patience. Ask the guy on the plane or in the next office about his kids and you will make a friend. You will also find that what goes around comes around.

Give a Helping Hand to the Next Guy

When you connect with new fathers you know or meet, don't be shy about telling them what you have learned as a dad. You can also pass on what you have learned to other rookie dads by taking your baby to a Boot Camp workshop or posting your comments on DadsAdventure.com. Ask your questions as well, and hear what the experience of other fathers has taught them. Get some fathers you know together for a hike or trip to the car show and try to make it a regular habit.

Look Forward to Organized Activities with Other Dads

Sports generally start at age 5 (soccer, T-Ball) and offerings like flag football and lacrosse are continually being added. The YMCA's Guides and Princesses father and son/daughter programs also start when your child is about 5. They all provide great opportunities for dads in coaching, leading and contributing, and you should look forward to the camaraderie that can develop as dads work together and learn from each other. Some men who have never played sports themselves end up becoming their child's coach and the neighborhood's as well. This can be a great way to go as a dad.

Let's Make the World a Better Place for All Our Children

You do your job, and your brothers, cousins and friends (and eventually your own sons) will notice and follow. If we all do our jobs, we will be leaving the world that our kids inherit in better shape than we found it. Not a bad legacy.

Fatherhood presents each of us a tremendous opportunity. Let's help each other make the most of it.

> " When men facing a common challenge get together, a locker room bond quickly develops and they come away inspired."
> — Veteran Dad

Welcome to Serious Manhood

Conducting Boot Camp for New Dads for more than two decades and raising four children of my own has given me plenty of time to think about what it means to be a father and what it takes to be a dad. Many men fail their children in many ways, and in my day job of working with Trauma Centers across the U.S., I see some of the saddest results in pediatric intensive care units. I ask myself, what causes a man to fail as a father when virtually every one of us wants to do right by our child? What do men who are just starting out need to know to do their best?

As men, our stereotyped desire is being seen as attractive, sexually active and successful with women. Pick up any men's magazine: in keeping with the fantasy, among the articles on six pack abs and turning her into a nymph, you will be hard pressed to find any evidence any of us are married, or worse, tied down with children. So while we still buy the magazines (hey, it's a fantasy), we know better.

The reality is that we men broadly report that being seen as honorable, resourceful and respected is much more important to our sense of manhood. Before our child arrives, we have already learned that having one woman who cares deeply for us, loving her, protecting her, having her belong to us and us to her, knowing she can count on us no matter what, is a great feeling that brings out the best in us as men.

> " You have an idea of what it is to be a dad and then being a dad happens to you. You have NO idea."
>
> — Veteran Dad

Next comes the big leap – a child, fatherhood and family, with our mate turning into a mom – and we run into another stereotype: the notion that fatherhood is emasculating, that becoming a father, with all that diaper changing, baby talk, and nurturing, somehow makes us less of a man. And we learn otherwise.

So to all new fathers who give it their best:
It takes a man to raise a child. Staying up with a crying baby, working without sleep, changes in our relationship with our mates, needing to earn more and still do our part at home, rarely time for ourselves, and the demands of protecting, guiding, and being a role model to our children.

Among fathers, the real man walks his crying baby night after night even though exhausted, cares for his baby's mom with little in return, helps his son get to college when he didn't go himself, volunteers as his daughter's coach even though he doesn't know what to do, fights to get help for his sick child from a system that doesn't care, and forges ahead with a troubled teenager when he doesn't have a clue.

Fatherhood presents all of us, no matter our size, strength or income, a unique opportunity to show what we are made of, and to be a hero to someone we love. Hard to imagine, but you are going to be a hero; the tough kind that takes decades, with times when you may want to walk away. The kind that takes the special courage of having to answer to no one but yourself. The kind that takes care of his child no matter what.

When she is born, she will wrap her tiny hand around your little finger – and before you know it, you will be wrapped around hers. He will fall asleep on your chest, warm and secure in your arms, with no one else to look after him and protect him like you will.

As she learns to walk, you will be there to catch her when she falls. When he learns to talk, his first words will include daddy – or something close enough. When she scores a goal, she will look right at you and smile.

And when he graduates, he will grab you in a bear hug and not say a word.

On behalf of all veteran dads, I wish you strength and fortune in meeting the challenges ahead and experiencing the best that life has to offer. Welcome to the adventure of your life.

Welcome to serious manhood!

Notes

Notes

Notes

Notes